FLOWER AND PLANT PRODUCTION

in the Greenhouse

Fourth Edition

FLOWER AND PLANT

by

Kennard S. Nelson, Ph.D.

Florconsult
Columbus, Ohio

PRODUCTION

in the Greenhouse

INTERSTATE PUBLISHERS, INC.

Danville, Illinois

**FLOWER AND PLANT PRODUCTION
IN THE GREENHOUSE**

Fourth Edition

Order from

Interstate Publishers, Inc.
510 North Vermilion Street, P.O. Box 50
Danville, IL 61834-0050
Phone: (800) 843-4774
Fax: (217) 446-9706

Library of Congress Catalog Card No. 88-82075

ISBN 0-8134-2843-2 (paperbound)
ISBN 0-8134-2891-2 (casebound)

3
4 5 6
7 8 9

PREFACE

The current effects of flower and plant distributing and marketing on greenhouse production in the United States and Canada are very different from what they were when this text was first published. Local greenhouse businesses now compete with distant ones on this and other continents.

Flower and Plant Production in the Greenhouse, Fourth Edition, is written for students and others who are interested in entering the business of flower and plant production. They need information about (1) relationships with other flower and plant businesses; (2) plants — how they grow and the surroundings that they require; (3) how people work with plants; (4) ways that various crops can fit in production space and can supply market demand; and (5) current sources of information from individuals, associations, periodicals, and other literature.

Although the emphasis remains on timeless subjects such as plants — their growth, their relationships to surroundings, and growers' methods for working with them, new material has been added in this edition on the effects of distribution and transportation on producing and marketing greenhouse flowers and plants; reference to the United States and Canada combined as the domestic area; consideration of greenhouse producing and marketing as a business operation; sources of the latest information about constantly changing subjects like pest and pathogen controls, manufactured growth regulators, fertilizers, and greenhouse buildings and equipment; details on careers; new, up-to-date illustrations; and an expanded, cross-referenced index for easy access of information by the student.

Kennard S. Nelson
Columbus, Ohio

CONTENTS

Chapter 1

FLOWER AND PLANT PRODUCING AND MARKETING

Flowers and ornamental plants may be produced in greenhouses or outdoors, depending on the kinds of plants, the climate, and the season of the year. Because of climate, some geographical locations are better suited than others for production. Regardless of production location and conditions, the products may be distributed and marketed through the same systems.

Generally, air and land transportation is widely available, rapid, and within economic means; because of this, the products marketed locally may be grown locally or at distant places, domestic or foreign. For example, the floriculture products purchased by a Circleville, Ohio, resident may have been grown in these locations: carnation in Colombia, South America; chrysanthemum pot plant in Springfield, Ohio; lily cut flower in Holland; foliage plants in Florida or Costa Rica; rose cut flower in Columbus, Ohio; begonia pot plant in Ontario, Canada; and orchid cut flower in Hawaii.

The plants and flowers purchased by a customer in Sudbury, Ontario, may have similar domestic and foreign origins.

The text of this book is concerned with producing and marketing flowers and ornamental plants in the United States and Canada. The conduct of these businesses is affected by their competitors—both indoor and outdoor, on this and other continents.

PRODUCING

The United States and Canada

Pot plants.—There is general greenhouse production of pot-plant crops throughout the United States and Canada. In addition, there are concentrations of foliage-plant production in the southern United States and of flowering pot-plant crops in the southwestern and southern United States. Some pot-plant production in the South is outdoors under plastic screen and in greenhouses that are not fully equipped.

Cut flowers.—Rose flowers are produced in greenhouses throughout the United States and Canada, but the production of other cut flowers is concentrated in the southwestern and southern United States. There also are large areas of rose-flower greenhouse production in the southwestern United States.

Some flower crops are produced outdoors or under plastic screen in the southwestern and southern United States. Spray chrysanthemum and gladiolus are grown that way in the South, and statice, daisy, and baby's breath are also grown that way in the Southwest.

Other Areas

Plant and flower quality and quantity can be expected to be better in climates of uniform sunlight and temperature. Also, low-cost production may be possible because less heating and cooling are required and greenhouses need not be so fully equipped. The geographical locations with that kind of climate are closer to the equator for uniform sunlight and have satisfactory temperature because of land elevation or surrounding water.

There is much production of foliage plants outdoors and under plastic screen in the Caribbean islands and in Central America.

Cut flowers.—Cut-flower crops may be produced with only protection from moisture in some areas of South America, Mexico, and Kenya. Cut-flower crops may also be exported from Southern Hemisphere areas like Australia, South America, and South Africa because of the better climate in their opposite seasons of the year.

MARKETING

Producers also are marketers. They have to sell their produce in some way. If their customers are wholesalers or retailers, they are producers who are wholesale marketers. If their customers are consumers, they are producers who are retail marketers. The producers who sell directly to consumers may buy plants and flowers from other growers or wholesalers and may operate flower shops in addition to their production businesses.

The plant and flower producers who market locally to wholesalers or to retailers may sell and deliver their products to wholesale stores, flower shops, garden stores, general-merchandise stores, and interiorscape services. If the individual plant- and flower-production business is established for long-distance marketing, the selling may be done either directly to customers or to shippers who then ship to customers.

There are various marketing and distribution routes for plants and flowers.

Wholesaling

Types of wholesale marketing that may be involved in the United States and Canada are wholesale store, shipper, producer-to-producer, broker, and auction.

Wholesale stores.—The main products marketed in wholesale stores are usually cut flowers. Various types of pot plants and florists' supplies may also be sold. The plants and flowers are purchased from growers and shippers. The florists' supplies are purchased from manufacturers or from manufacturers' representatives.

The customers are retailers.

Shipper.—Shippers are wholesalers who are located in areas of

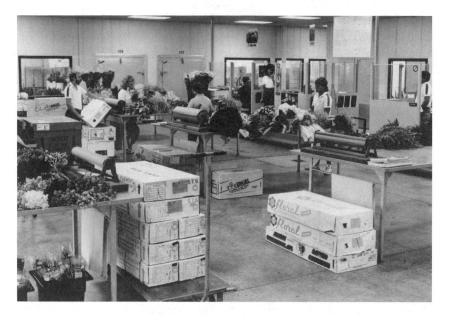

Fig. 1-1. Wholesale store cut-flower sales.

Fig. 1-2. Wholesale store florist-supplies sales.

concentrated production. They buy flowers and plants from growers or through auctions for sale and shipment to wholesalers and retailers. Shippers may buy from only one producer, or they may consolidate orders from various producers for single shipments.

Producer-to-producer.—This type of wholesaling occurs mainly among pot-plant producers who buy and sell among themselves to supplement the kind or amount of plants available for their customers.

Brokers.—Broker marketing is often used with foliage and crop-starter plants. Customers are plant and flower producers. Brokers list available plants, and their traveling salespeople place orders with the suppliers, who ship directly to customers. Suppliers bill brokers, and brokers bill customers.

Auctions.—There are not many auctions in the United States and Canada, and they are located only in areas of concentrated production. Auctions usually are cooperatively owned and operated by plant and flower producers. The main customers are shippers.

Retailing

Retail marketing is done by flower shops, general-merchandise stores, garden stores, interiorscape services, flower boutiques, and bucket stands.

Flower shops.—Usually something is added to plants and flowers in flower shops. Trims are added to larger plants, and smaller plants are grouped in gardens. Flowers are arranged or used in various designs. Glassware, ribbons, and pottery are used to improve display of plants and flowers.

Weddings, funerals, and festive occasions are serviced. Interiorscaping may be included.

Manufactured plants and flowers are used in addition to living plants and flowers.

Most flower shops have the capability of taking orders for floral products to be presented as consumers desire in almost any part of the world.

Flower shops usually offer credit and delivery service.

Fig. 1-3. Flower shop with attached display greenhouse.

Fig. 1-4. Flower shop interior.

General-merchandise stores.—The extent of plant and flower marketing varies considerably among general-merchandise stores. Some stores have floral departments that are comparable to flower shops. Other stores may be in the floral business only with pot plants appropriate for the season or for holidays.

Usually general-merchandise stores do not offer credit and delivery service.

Fig. 1-5. Flower and plant department in a supermarket.

Garden stores.—Garden stores typically market some foliage plants year-round, pot plants for holidays and special occasions, and garden plants in season.

Garden stores do not usually extend delivery or credit to their customers.

Interiorscape service.—Interiorscape services may include the use of flowering and foliage plants in homes, offices, restaurants, public buildings, and malls. The charge for the service usually includes design, plants, planting, other ornamentals, and maintenance.

Fig. 1-6. Garden store interior-plant department.

Flower boutiques.—Flower boutiques may be located in shopper high-traffic areas like malls, transportation terminals, and near department store exits. The products are usually limited to easily transported items like small pot plants, gardens, and flower bouquets.

Bucket stands.—Bucket stands usually have flowers in buckets of water. The flowers are sold singly or in mixed bouquets. The stands may be located at street corners, in store-front buildings, or included in the sales rooms of flower shops or general-merchandise stores.

ESTABLISHING AND OPERATING GREENHOUSE BUSINESSES

All greenhouse businesses have about the same types of activities and need the same sort of information for operating them. The needs for organization, money, and suppliers, however, vary mainly with the size of the business.

Fig. 1-7. Interiorscape in an office building.

Size

The size of a greenhouse area may vary from about 20,000 square feet to over 1,000,000 square feet. Some floriculture businesses have field as well as greenhouse crop areas.

The type of marketing also affects the size of the business. Wholesale or retail marketing that includes marketing of plants, flowers, and supplies from other sources can greatly increase the size of the business.

Organization

Regardless of the size of the business, the owner sets policy and makes decisions about capital investments. If the business is small, the owner is also directly involved in various aspects of managing, like hiring, assigning work, directing associates, setting wages, and promoting or firing. Owners need one or more managers for larger greenhouse businesses. The number of people needed for operating greenhouse businesses of various sizes may be:

Greenhouse Area	People[1]
½ acre	owner and family
1 acre	owner, family, 1 or 2 associates
2 acres	owner, 1 manager, 6 associates
5 acres	owner, 3 managers, 30 associates
10 acres	owner, 4 managers, 100 associates

Activities

The activities in greenhouse businesses can generally be classified as producing, marketing, maintaining, accounting, and transporting. In small greenhouses, individual owners may handle all activities. However, as the businesses grow in size, specialist associates and managers are needed to get the job done.

Producing.—The producing activities involve plants and the adjustment of surroundings. Usually these producing activities are intertwined and concurrent, rather than separate and isolated. For example, although the activity is planting, heat and ventilation are adjusted as needed during planting. Some activities with plants are propagating; planting; pinching and pruning; applying pesticides, fungicides, and growth regulators; and harvesting.

---

[1]The number of people involved varies mainly with the capability of the family members, the type of crops, and the type of marketing.

Adjusting-surroundings activities may include heating and ventilating, irrigating, and applying fertilizer.

Marketing.—Marketing activities vary mainly with the type of product, the location of greenhouse, and the size of business. When the product is locally grown and marketed pot plants, the producer may market to wholesalers who operate either stores or routes. Then the main activities are making sales by telephone and delivering plants to wholesalers. If the pot plants are marketed to retailers, there will be more telephone and delivery activities.

Pot-plant producers who market their plants long distances may handle the sales themselves and then ship by (1) trucks under their control, (2) common carriers—either trucks or airplanes, and (3) shippers. Or, they may sell to shippers who handle both sales and shipping.

Greenhouse operators who produce flowers for local sales may either market them to wholesale stores or establish their own wholesale store. Sales of flowers to other wholesale stores require telephone sales and delivery to stores, but individual establishment of a wholesale store requires capital investment, the hiring of salespeople, and the purchase of other flowers and supplies.

Producers who market cut flowers long distances either handle sales and ship by common carrier or sell the flowers to shippers who do both sales and shipping. In some areas, the flowers are delivered to auction for selling.

Producers of crop starters may do the selling also or use brokers. The crop starters are usually shipped by common carrier.

Maintaining.—Much maintenance work in greenhouse businesses is done by associates in the firm. There are activities like heat generation and distribution; water distribution; repair of equipment and vehicles; and minor construction, including construction of walks and benches.

Accounting.—This is the process of accumulating the results of business transactions so business analysis can be made and business reports can be prepared.

Transporting.—The transporting of products and materials within the organization is usually done by production and maintenance people.

Delivery and route sales are handled by individuals who are licensed for the vehicles that are used.

Money

Owners and associates have mutual interests in the financial success of their firms.

Owners have to have or be able to borrow enough money to start a business, and they have to operate the business so there is enough cash flow to maintain the property and to pay for purchases and operating costs. At the end of the accounting period, the amount of money collected has to be greater than the amount of money spent.

Investment.—The business investment is for land, buildings, and equipment. Even for a small greenhouse production business, the money required can be a few hundred-thousand dollars. This is more money than most individuals have, so borrowing is required, and the prospective greenhouse operator and the banker have to be satisfied that the planned business has a good chance of repaying the loan plus interest.

The discussion with the banker must also include funds for the operation of the business until plants and flowers are ready for sale—a period of several months to a few years. The need for start-up funds is common for all types of business, but the amount of money and the length of the loaning period vary with the type of business.

Usually the total amount of money for business investment is needed immediately. Loans for land and building often are long-term; payments are made for 25 years or more. Loans for equipment may be for terms of three to five years. The money for start-up operation is needed at regular intervals; loans may be for terms of about three years.

Floriculture businesses that are involved solely in marketing usually do not require as much start-up money as production businesses. Marketing does not require as much land nor as many buildings, reducing the initial investment. Because these operations purchase plants and flowers and immediately sell them, there is no delay between opening for business and receiving income from sales.

Operating.—All businesses are concerned with cash flow. Money has to flow in as rapidly as it flows out, or bills—and wages—cannot be paid without borrowing. Businesses have fixed costs, like land, buildings, equipment, and wages, that do not vary from month to month. The sales in plant- and flower-production businesses are not nearly so well fixed. For example, pot-plant growers may have large crop-starter costs during the summer and fall for anticipated sales in December, April, and May. Rose-flower growers have reduced production and sales during the summer because plants are cut back and during the late fall through early winter because additional plants are pinched to produce a Valentine's Day crop.

Income.—Income is sometimes called "profit" or "the bottom line." It is what may be left after all the bills are paid for the accounting period. Owners have to work constantly for greater sales and smaller costs so there will be some income. That is the only way they can stay in business.

Associates.—The first concerns of associates have to be the type of work and the surroundings. Is the type of work of real, personal interest and enjoyment? By being on the job, can they make a measurable contribution to the company? Are business and living surroundings desirable for themselves and their families? If the answers are yes, then wage and other benefits may be considered.

With no specific schooling or experience, the entering associate should expect entry-level wage—maybe no more than federal minimum wage, but this should not be of concern at the moment. It is important to learn at the time of hiring what the wage limits are for the job and at what intervals wage-increase or release evaluations are made. The first evaluation will probably be made about one month after hiring, and for the good of the individual and the company, the associate either will be offered an increase in pay or will be released. Evaluations for further wage increase may be made in about one year.

An individual with favorable schooling and experience can expect to start at a higher entry wage, but top wage for the job will be the same as for inexperienced applicants. Evaluations for wage increase will probably be made at one month and about one year after hiring.

Managers and salespeople entering employment will probably receive a base salary plus a commission based on increase in production or sales. That type of compensation automatically adjusts to the results of the work.

Whether on wage or salary, it is important for each associate to properly evaluate the worth of the other benefits, like profit sharing, medical service, and insurance. The monetary value of these benefits can be of considerable worth.

Pay for the same job at the company may be expected to increase only if sales and production increase. If sales and production remain about the same, increase in pay may be possible only if there is a job with more responsibility open in the company. If there are no openings in the company, it may be necessary to seek a more responsible job at another floriculture company.

Suppliers

Greenhouse businesses use local suppliers whenever possible, but many items can be supplied only by specialist firms, wherever they are located. The contact with specialist firms may be by mail, by telephone, or by traveling salespeople. The traveling salespeople may be members of the supply firm, members of brokerage firms, or manufacturers' representatives.

Brokerage firms are called **brokers**. They are sales representatives of producing or manufacturing companies. They acquaint customers with the products and place orders with producing firms. The producer ships directly to customers, and the broker bills the customers. Broker firms also supply literature, scheduling, and other services. Brokers usually represent various producing and manufacturing companies whose products may be needed by their customers.

Traveling salespeople for supply firms represent only their producing or manufacturing company. They acquaint customers with their products and place orders with their firms. Shipping and billing is done by their supply firms. Producing-manufacturing firms also supply customers with literature, scheduling, and other services.

Traveling salespeople who are called **manufacturers' representatives** usually represent more than one manufacturer. They acquaint customers with the products and place orders with the manufacturers, who then ship directly to and bill customers. The manufacturers pay commission to the representatives for whatever they sell.

Crop starters.—Garden-plant seed is usually purchased from brokers, but large quantities of seed may be purchased directly from seed producers.

Rose plants are bought from the traveling salespeople employed by the plant-producing companies.

Bulbs and many crop starters for pot plants are bought from either producers or brokers.

Chrysanthemum and carnation crop starters may be purchased from either producers or brokers. Sellers of chrysanthemum cuttings also provide scheduling for those crops.

Plants for resale.—Foliage plants may be purchased directly from southern producers or from brokers. Shipments may be for a truckload or a smaller quantity. Foliage-plant trucking firms consolidate orders so that plants ordered from various producers will be shipped on the same truck.

Mature flowering pot plants may be purchased directly from producers or from shippers or truckers. The shippers and truckers usually consolidate orders from various producers.

Production supplies.—Items from local suppliers may be general agricultural fertilizers, pipe and fittings, general hardware, heating equipment, hose, lighting, cultivators, and hand tools.

Items from manufacturers or specialty suppliers include peat moss, containers, cooling equipment, support networks, lighting, transport, irrigation, pesticides, fungicides, growth regulators, fertilizers, fertilizer injectors, and labels.

Supplies for resale.—Producer-marketers who include a whole-sale store in their marketing may sell floral supplies as well as cut flowers and pot plants. Thousands of items like vases, ribbons, cards, silk flowers and foliage, and design foams may be stocked. These items may be purchased from manufacturers' representatives or directly from manufacturers' salespeople.

Information Sources

Schools.—The types of schools for floriculture training are high-school vocational, trade, two-year college, and four-year college. Some trade schools and two-year colleges include commercial work experience as part of the training. Many students gain valuable information by working part-time at floriculture businesses while in school.

Bookkeeping and accounting training may be taken in high schools and in business and trade schools.

Trade periodicals.—There are some trade periodicals for each type of floriculture business.

The following publications for greenhouse flower- and plant-production businesses are published monthly. These publications contain advertisements and current articles about growing.

Canadian Florist Greenhouse and Industry
109 Aerowood Drive, Unit 1
Mississauga, Ontario L4W 1Y5

Greenhouse Grower
37841 Euclid Avenue
Willoughby, OH 44094

Greenhouse Manager
120 St. Louis Avenue
Fort Worth, TX 76104

Grower Talks
250 Town Road
West Chicago, IL 60185

The Society of American Florists (SAF), 1601 Duke Street, Alexandria, VA 22214, is the national association for all branches of floriculture businesses. The SAF monthly publication is *Business News for the Floral Industry*. SAF members receive the publication with their membership. Nonmembers may subscribe to the publication.

Wholesale Florists & Florist Suppliers of America, Inc. (WF & FSA), 5313 Lee Highway, Arlington, VA 22207, is the national association for that branch of floriculture business. Its trade publication, *Link*, is published 10 times per year. WF & FSA members receive *Link* with their membership. Nonmembers may subscribe to this publication.

The following monthly publication is for interiorscaping businesses:

Interior Landscape Industry
111 N. Canal Street
Chicago, IL 60606

Two national associations have monthly publications for their specific crops. Members receive the publications with their memberships.

Florida Foliage Association
Box Y
Apopka, FL 32704

Roses, Inc.
Box 99
Haslett, MI 48840

Some of the wire services for retail florists have trade periodicals.

Florist is published monthly for members of Florists' Transworld Delivery, Box 2227, Southfield, MI 48037.

Flowers is published monthly for members of Teleflora, 12233 W. Olympic Boulevard, Los Angeles, CA 90064. Nonmembers may subscribe to this publication.

The Professional Floral Designer is published six times per year for members of American Floral Services, Inc., Box 12309, Oklahoma City, OK 73157. Nonmembers may subscribe to this publication.

Governmental and trade services.—The Cooperative Extension Service in the United States is funded and staffed by federal, state, and county governments to disseminate information about various branches of agriculture. Cooperative Extension Service offices are listed in telephone directories under the county listing. Among their services are publications, educational meetings, and visits from their specialists.

Each type of floriculture business may have state or province associations that publish bulletins monthly or periodically and that have yearly meetings for discussion of educational and business topics. Trade fairs may also be included. Sometimes these associations include all types of floriculture businesses as members.

In many metropolitan areas, there are plant and flower producer and retail florist associations. These associations may include both producers and retailers, or there may be separate associations for each type of business. Typically they meet monthly to discuss and act on common interests and problems. Usually some social activities are included.

Suppliers.—The firms and salespeople who provide merchandise for floriculture businesspeople may also provide valuable services like catalogs and literature, crop-production scheduling, marketing methods, and relationships within the industry. Some of the help from suppliers may be with money matters—either in extension of long-term credit or in advice on business procedures that allow timely collection of accounts receivable, which in turn allows greenhouse operators to receive discounts for paying their own accounts promptly.

Bankers.—Floriculture-business operators have continuing needs for advice from bankers. The banker who provides checking, savings, and loaning services is also a good source of information about general money matters.

Auditors.—The accounting procedures for the firm have to be established and maintained so that revenue and expense for crop and activity can be compared with previous periods. Owners and accountants need to communicate well so that the records allow filing of reports and provide the information the owners need to make business decisions.

Chapter 2

PLANTS

Greenhouse operators need a good understanding of plants and how they grow. It becomes second nature with greenhouse people to provide the surroundings that allow excellent growth of plants and flowers year-round.

Plants, like animals, have life, but there are many significant differences between plants and animals. Some characteristics of plants are (1) immobility, (2) food manufacturing, (3) change from vegetative to reproductive growth, (4) vegetative reproduction, and (5) bisexuality.

EXTERNAL APPEARANCES

Some of the most obvious features of plants are that they have stems, leaves, and roots—and that they do grow.

Stems

Plant stems are segmented, and the joining place of segments is called a *node.* There are underground as well as aboveground stems.

Nodes. —In aboveground stems, leaves develop from nodes, producing typical leafy stems. Shoots also may develop at nodes, and these shoots may be called *lateral stems,* or *branches.* Flowers may also

**Fig. 2-1. Chrysanthemum stem.
Leaves develop at stem nodes.**

develop from nodes. These *lateral flowers* have rather long, leafless stems.

Underground stems also have nodes, but they do not directly produce leaves, shoots, and flowers. The four types of underground stems are *bulb, corm, tuber,* and *rhizome.*

Bulbs have a sole, small, compact stem that is enclosed by fleshy scales. The greenhosue crops started from bulbs are Easter lily, tulip, daffodil, and hyacinth. The tips of the bulbs are somewhat pointed, and the bases are flat or rounded. After planting, roots develop from the base of the bulb, and eventually the growing stem emerges through the tip of the bulb.

Fig. 2-2. Gloxinia internodes are so short that leaves and flowers hide the plant stem from view.

Corms are shaped somewhat like bulbs, but they are solid rather than scaled. Several buds develop at the nodes of corms. After planting, roots develop from the base of the corm, and shoot growth starts from the topmost bud. With some kinds of plants or in certain conditions, shoot growth may develop from more than one bud. Crops started from corms are crocus and gladiolus.

Tuber shapes generally are oval rather than globular. Crops started from tubers may be gloxinia, caladium, and some begonia. Shoot growth is from the topmost bud. Caladium growers may scoop or score the topmost bud so growth starts from several lateral buds.

Rhizome underground stems generally grow horizontally, and

roots and shoots develop from nodes. Some rhizomes, like calla, may be large and coarse, while others, like ferns, may have a small diameter and be uniform.

Fig. 2-3. Easter lily bulb. The compact stem is enclosed by large scales.

Leaves. — There is much variability in leaf size, shape, and color. It is possible to identify the kind of plant just by examining the leaves. The most prominent part of a leaf is called the *blade.* Leaf blades of some plants, like carnation, develop directly from stems. When leaves are stalked, like geranium, the stalk is called a *petiole.* If there are more than one blade per petiole, the blades are called *leaflets.* Greenhouse rose plants have three- and five-leaflet leaves.

Flowers. — The origin of flowers in stems may be either terminal, like chrysanthemum, hydrangea, and rose, or lateral, like African violet, geranium, and petunia. The flowers per stem may be solitary, like rose, daffodil, and iris, or they may be in flower clusters, like chrysanthemum, Easter lily, and snapdragon. The individual flowers in a cluster may be called *florets.* In marketing, the term *flower* is used for cluster flowers as well as for solitary flowers.

Terminal and lateral flowers differ in place of origin and type of growth. In the kinds of plants that have a sole terminal flower, the flower develops in the stem tip as the growth in length changes from stem and leaf development to flower development. In the kinds of plants that have more than one terminal flower, the additional flowers develop at nodes just below the stem tip. Terminal flowers have leafy flower stems.

In the kinds of plants that have lateral flowers, the stem tip continues to develop stem and leaves, and the lateral flowers develop at nodes below the stem tip. Lateral flowers have leafless stems.

There are two general types of flower clusters: (1) *racemose*, which has an indeterminate type of flower development—the lower or outer florets develop first, and the upper or inner florets develop last and (2) *cymose*, which has a determinate type of floret development—the

Fig. 2-4. Some differences in leaf characteristics. Top row, left to right: pilea, azalea, chrysanthemum, schefflera, and snapdragon. Bottom row, left to right: rose, carnation, and geranium.

upper or inner florets develop first, and the lower or outer florets develop last.

There are various forms of racemose flower clusters. Their names and examples are (1) *head,* chrysanthemum, cineraria, marigold, zinnia; (2) *raceme,* Easter lily, fuchsia, hyacinth; (3) *spike,* snapdragon; and (4) *umbel,* azalea.

Cyme is the form of cymose flower clusters. Some of the cyme clusters are African violet, geranium, hydrangea, kalanchoe, and poinsettia.

The showy parts of flowers often are *petals,* but there are notable exceptions. The showy parts in poinsettia are bracts; in chrysanthemum, florets; and in hydrangeas, sepals.

Flowers contain the sexual parts of plants. Many kinds of plants are *bisexual,* meaning that the flowers have both male and female parts. African violet, azalea, and petunia are examples of bisexual flowers. Chrysanthemum, cineraria, and marigold have *unisexual* female flowers as well as bisexual flowers. Begonia, calla, and poinsettia have both male and female unisexual flowers on each plant.

Colors.—Green is the predominant color of plants. Plants appear green because a pigment in plant tissues absorbs other-color light and reflects green light. This pigment is called *chlorophyll.* It does more than give color to plants. Chlorophyll is part of the food-manufacturing system in plants. Other colors of plants are caused by different pigments. When plant parts have more than one color, they are *variegated.*

Seed.—Seed can result from sexual activities within flowers, but floriculture plants and flowers are marketed before seed production starts. The production of seed is a specialty business in which plants are grown for that purpose.

Roots

Roots have continuous growth. They are not segmented. Roots are most often underground. Roots do branch, and some kinds of plants do have enlarged roots that appear similar to some underground stems. The enlarged roots may be called *tubers.* Roots do not have nodes, and leaves and flowers do not develop directly from roots.

Fig. 2-5. An incurved standard or commercial chrysanthemum flower (Yoder Bros., Inc., photograph).

Fig. 2-6. A spider chrysanthemum flower (Yoder Bros., Inc., photograph).

Fig. 2-7. A pompon spray chrysanthemum flower (Yoder Bros., Inc., photograph).

Fig. 2-8. A decorative spray chrysanthemum flower (Yoder Bros., Inc., photograph).

Fig. 2-9. A single spray chrysanthemum flower (Yoder Bros., Inc., photograph).

Fig. 2-10. An anemone spray chrysanthemum flower (Yoder Bros., Inc., photograph).

Fig. 2-11. African violet lateral cyme flowers.

Fig. 2-12. Male (stamen) and female (pistil) parts of an Easter-lily flower.

Fig. 2-13. Poinsettia flowers are small and yellow. The large, showy bracts are immediately below the flowers.

Growth

Plant stems and roots increase in length by formation of cells in stem and root tips and by enlargement of these cells. As aboveground stems increase in length, stems and leaves develop. The plants may have either *single-stem* type of growth or *selfbranching* type of growth with bushlike plant development.

Fig. 2-14. Root growth of a young begonia plant.

Fig. 2-15. Selfbranching growth of an exacum plant.

Plants may also have limited growth in leafy-stem length that terminates in the development of flowers, or they may have unlimited growth in leafy-stem length. The limited type of stem growth that terminates with flowers is called *determinate* growth. Carnation, chrysanthemum, and rose are examples of single-stem determinate growth, and cineraria and exacum are examples of selfbranching determinate growth.

Geranium, petunia, and African violet are examples of *indeterminate* growth. The stem continues to increase in length, and the flowers develop laterally.

With plants that have single-stem determinate growth, shoots do develop laterally after flower formation in the stem tip. For several nodes below the terminal flower, the lateral shoots also terminate with flowers. The stems of these lateral flowers are short, but they vary in length, ranging from no stem for the shoot just below the terminal flower to the longest stem for the lowest lateral flower that develops. The shoots that develop at lower nodes will be leafy.

With some of the crops that have single-stem determinate growth, greenhouse operators pinch the stems early in growth. Lateral shoots then develop, causing bushy growth and more stems for terminal flowering later.

Roots and shoots develop when seed is placed in warm and moist propagating surroundings. This start in growth from seed is known as *germination.*

When a stem tip is placed in warm and moist propagating surroundings, roots form from the basal part, and the young plant is an exact duplicate of the parent plant. Exact duplicates can also develop when stem segments, leaves, or small parts of stems are used in propagating.

Although the new plants resulting from vegetative propagation usually are exactly the same as the parent plant, occasionally change in some heritable character may occur in the part being propagated. The new plant then would not be exactly the same as the parent plant but would include whatever change occurred in the part used in propagation. If the change is favorable, further propagation may be only from the changed plant. Such a sudden change is called *mutation.* Growth changes like this may occur at any stage of plant development, and the change involves only a part of the plant. If new plants with this changed heritage are to be reproduced, vegetative propagation

Fig. 2-16. Indeterminate growth of geranium. The stem continues to grow as flowers develop laterally.

must be made only from the changed part of the plant. Many floriculture plants are selections of mutations that occurred naturally.

Mutations can also be caused by the use of certain chemicals and radiation on plants. Plant breeders often use mutant selection in their work.

PLANT NAMES

The proper names used for plants refer to classification according to specific plant characteristics. These names are also called **botanical** or **scientific.** Plants also have common names that do not necessarily indicate relationship to proper names. Some examples are:

Common Name	Proper Name
African violet	*Saintpaulia ionantha*
azalea	*Rhododendron hybrida*
chrysanthemum	*Chrysanthemum morifolium*
daffodil	*Narcissus pseudonarcissus*
geranium	*Pelargonium hortorum*
Easter lily	*Lilium longiflorum*
petunia	*Petunia hybrida*
rose	*Rosa hybrida*

Plant common names are usually used in this book.

INTERNAL CONDITIONS

The building units of plants are cells, and as cells multiply, various tissues and characteristic plant parts develop. This growth requires food and a suitable supply of materials from plant surroundings.

Food

Green plants manufacture food. All of the floriculture plants are green and have the capability of making food when they are in suitable surroundings. The process of food manufacturing by green plants is called **photosynthesis.** Chlorophyll in plants is involved in photosynthesis, and the requirements from plant surroundings are satisfactory amounts of carbon dioxide, water, light, and heat. Sugar is the product of photosynthesis.

Uses of Food

The sugar that is made in plants may be used within the plants in three ways: (1) it may be converted to other compounds, (2) it may be accumulated, or (3) it may be consumed. The other materials that sugar may be converted to may be protein, fats, starches, and other necessary materials in plants. The conversion of sugar to other materials is called *assimilation.*

Some conversion of sugar results in the formation of materials called *hormones.* They are growth regulators that may affect branching, flowering, and stem curvature. Stem curvature is called *tropism. Phototropism* is the term for stem curvature caused by light. Carnation and Easter lily are examples of plants whose stems curve in the direction of the light source. Because of this stem curvature, carnation plants cause more weight on the light-source side of their support networks. And lily growers rotate lily plants regularly so stems grow upright.

Geotropism is the term for direction of root and stem growth in relation to force of gravity. Roots grow down, and stems generally grow up. When bulbs are planted upside down, the roots will still grow down,

Fig. 2-17. Carnation stem curvature toward light source (phototropism).

Fig. 2-18. Gladiolus and snapdragon curvature upwards(geotropism) after they were placed in a horizontal position for a few hours.

and the stem will make a U-curve and grow upward. The geotropism effect also occurs in cut flowers. When gladiolus and snapdragon are placed horizontally, either in shipping or in designs, the stem tips curve upward.

The sugar that is consumed within plants is converted to heat energy, water, and carbon dioxide. This is the same process as ***respiration*** in animals except there is no breathing action in plants. There must be an oxygen supply for respiration. The oxygen may come from within, because of photosynthesis, and from the surrounding air.

Entrance and Exit

Materials have to be in liquid, gas, or radiant form to enter or exit plants. Gaseous exchange is mainly by means of pores called ***stomates.*** Stomates are located mainly in leaves, and they have the capability of opening and closing. Exchange of liquid moisture and dissolved materials is mostly by root tips. Radiant exchange can be by means of various plant surfaces.

Fig. 2-19. The effects of amount of roots on plant growth. The lily plant at the left did not grow satisfactorily because of the lack of root growth in water-logged soil.

Moisture.—Moisture in gaseous form *(water vapor)* is exchanged mainly through stomates. Loss of water from plants is called *transpiration.* The rate of transpiration is greater when the surrounding air is dry. Plants wilt when moisture loss is greater than the amount of moisture entering the plant root tips.

Moisture in liquid form enters plants mainly at the root tips. When root tips are in active growth and the soil is moist, there will usually be entry of water into plants. Continuous root growth occurs only when there is an adequate supply of air in soils. When soils are constantly wet *(waterlogged),* the soil air supply is very low, and there will be very little new root growth and very little entry of water into plants, in spite of the plentiful amount of water in the soil.

Dissolved minerals.—Solids cannot enter plants until they are in the dissolved form. The chemical compounds of fertilizers are needed in plants for the conversion, together with sugar, into materials required for plant life and growth. When fertilizers are dissolved in water, the chemicals of the fertilizers are in the form that can enter plant root tips. Growers, however, have to be very careful about the amounts of fertilizers used. Excess amounts of fertilizers can cause death of roots, with the results that neither water nor fertilizer materials will be able to enter the plants.

Carbon dioxide.—The main place of entry of carbon dioxide into plants is through stomates, and the time of entry usually is during daylight or when high-intensity lighting is used. Internal supplies of carbon dioxide are depleted then because of photosynthesis. The natural amount of carbon dioxide in outdoor air is generally satisfactory for plant growth if greenhouse ventilation allows daily exchange with outdoor air.

If there are variations in the amount of carbon dioxide in the air surrounding plants, there would also be variations in the amount of carbon dioxide entering plants. Carbon dioxide reductions can be expected to limit food manufacture, and additional amounts of carbon dioxide should increase the amount of food made. If greenhouse ventilation is restricted in cold weather, there may be a shortage of carbon dioxide for photosynthesis and a reduction in plant growth and development. For this reason, some growers add carbon dioxide to greenhouse air from fall to spring.

Oxygen.—Plant stomates are also the places for the exchange of oxygen between air and plants. Plants need oxygen continuously for respiration. During the day there is an oxygen source from within the plants because of photosynthesis. At night, the oxygen that is needed must enter the plants from the surrounding air. The amount of oxygen in greenhouse air generally is sufficient for plant needs unless heat or carbon dioxide generators without adequate outdoor air inlets are used in the greenhouses. Such depletion of oxygen may limit plant growth.

Air pollutants.—Pollutants may also enter plants through stomates. Some sources of air pollutants are heat and carbon dioxide generators, neighboring industries, herbicides, pesticides, motor vehicles, fruit, and decaying trash. Pollutants may cause plant disfigurement, malformed growth, and possibly death.

Light.—Light that contacts plants is reflected from the surfaces, or it enters through the plant surfaces. Pigments in plants affect the amount and kind of light that enters plants. More light enters dark-colored tissues than white and light-colored tissues. Light that enters plants may convert to heat or may be involved in photosynthesis and hormone activities.

Heat.—There are exchanges of infrared radiation through plant surfaces. Entering rays cause an increase in plant temperature, and exiting rays cause a decrease in temperature.

There also are exchanges of heat between plants and the contacting air. The direction of heat transfer is from warm to cool.

SURROUNDINGS AND PLANT GROWTH

Plant growth and development are influenced by the combined effects of all parts of the surroundings. Greenhouse surroundings generally include light, heat, moisture, air, and minerals. Greenhouse operators choose cultivars that are suitable for the climate and season in which they will be grown.

Light

Some of the effects of excessive amounts of sunlight on plant growth may be (1) short, narrow, rigid stems; (2) small, thick leaves; (3) small flowers; (4) light-colored or bleached stems, leaves, and flowers; (5) early flowering of some crops and delayed flowering of others; and (6) the possibility of burned areas of leaves and flowers. Because of the direct relationship between the amount of sunlight and the resultant heat, the effects on plant growth may be caused by a combination of light and heat.

The effects of sunlight of low intensity and short duration on plant growth may be (1) slow rate of growth—longer crop time; (2) thin leaves; (3) small flowers; (4) dull-colored stems, leaves, and flowers. Again, because of the direct relationship between amount of sunlight and resultant heat, plant growth effects may be caused by a combination of light and heat.

In addition to the effects of the amount of light caused by sunlight intensity and duration, there are some specific plant-growth effects caused by the daily length of lighting *(photoperiod).* Chrysanthemum and poinsettia plants develop stems and leaves in long photoperiods and flowers in short photoperiods. Carnation plants can develop stems, leaves, and flowers in either long or short photoperiods, but flowering is more prompt in long photoperiods.

There are some relationships between amount of heat and photoperiods and some plant-growth effects. For example, petunia seedlings at temperatures above 55°F will remain single stem in long photoperiods but will branch when they are grown at that temperature in short photoperiods. At temperatures below 55°F, petunia seedlings will branch in either short or long photoperiods. To schedule Easter lily for Easter flowering, the bulbs are placed in temperatures lower than 50°F for a minimum time of six weeks, but the same effect on flowering can result when the bulbs are in cool temperatures for part of the time and then the plants, after shoot emergence, are supplied long photoperiods for the same length of time that was missed in cooling.

Heat

Various amounts of heat are used around greenhouse crops, depending on the type of growth that is needed. With bulbs like daffodil and Easter lily, cool temperatures (below 50°F) are maintained for several weeks because that causes earlier flowering. Iris bulbs need carefully scheduled periods of warm and cool temperatures to prepare them for short-period forcing. Azalea and hydrangea plants are placed in cool temperatures for several weeks after flower buds are formed because that causes prompt flowering during forcing.

Cut flowers and mature flowering pot plants are placed in cool temperatures after harvest because there is very little further growth and development at temperatures below 50°F.

The temperatures used during growth of greenhouse crops are within the limits of 50° to 85°F. Generally, soil temperatures of 70° to 75°F are used in propagating soils because seed germination and rooting of cuttings proceed faster in warm surroundings.

Moisture

Wilting is the apparent symptom of lack of water in plants, and signs of periodic water shortage are smaller leaves, shorter stems, and smaller flowers. Leaf color is gray-green rather than bright green.

Air

If there is a shortage of carbon dioxide in greenhouse air, general growth of plants can be slower and smaller.

Oxygen supply in greenhouse air usually is suitable for good plant growth. The common problem, however, is that the air supply in soil is limited, and then root growth also is limited because of lack of oxygen. Waterlogged soils lack air—including oxygen.

Minerals

The minerals that affect plant growth are the dissolved fertilizer materials that enter plants from the soil. Plant growth may be affected by (1) general lack of fertilizer, (2) general excess of fertilizer, (3) incorrect soil pH, and (4) lack of specific fertilizer.

Fig. 2-20. The increase in size of these leaves since the rooted mum cutting was planted indicates that all of the surroundings have been very satisfactory.

When there is general lack of fertilizer in the soil, plant growth is slow; leaves and shoots are small and pale-green; and plants are erect and rigid. When there is a general excess of fertilizer in the soil, there will be no new root growth, or the roots may actually die. Plant leaves droop and are dull-colored. Top growth of plants is very slow. Plants may die.

Many of the greenhouse crops grow satisfactorily when the soil pH is 6.0 to 6.5. When the soil pH is higher, the leaves may be generally yellow (chlorotic) rather than green. With some kinds of plants, the leaf veins may remain green and the areas among the veins yellow. If the soil pH is too low—possibly 4.0 or lower—roots and plants may die.

Chapter 3

BUILDINGS AND EQUIPMENT

Floriculture production businesses usually need some conventional buildings as well as greenhouse buildings. The conventional buildings that may be needed are similar to those used by various kinds of businesses for shipping, sales, accounting, and storage.

In order to provide suitable growing conditions for plants, greenhouse construction is very different from conventional-building construction. Greenhouses have to (1) admit the maximum amount of sunlight, (2) allow sufficient ventilation to exhaust the excessive heat caused by sunlight, and (3) provide for the supply and removal of large amounts of water. Greenhouses are constructed by contractors who specialize in that type of building.

There must be good access to the buildings for motor vehicles of any size. If regular shipping is involved, truck-level handling under cover is provided.

GREENHOUSE BUILDINGS

The transparent or translucent covering (walls, roof, and ends) is the most obvious feature of a greenhouse building. Greenhouses also have characteristic heating and ventilating systems, but they are not

Fig. 3-1. A flower and plant greenhouse business in Ohio that includes flower and plant producing and wholesale-store marketing.

so noticeable. There are several types of greenhouses, and the objectives in the choice of a greenhouse are to (1) provide the size and arrangement suitable for the crops to be grown, (2) allow good internal and external access, and (3) provide satisfactory sunlight, air, heat, and water.

The greenhouse parts that make the closure around the production area are the *framework* and the *covering.* The building is completed by the addition of ventilation, heating, electric power, and water supply and drainage. A framework to be covered by rigid material like glass has plane surfaces. A framework to be covered with flexible material like some plastics may have plane or curved surfaces.

Framework.—Greenhouse framework has to be sturdy enough to support the combined load of itself, attached equipment, covering, wind, and snow. The use of steel and aluminum members provides necessary strength as well as minimum blockage of sunlight transmission. There are variations, but framework members generally are (1) the *sideposts,* erected at each bay; (2) the *trusses,* fastened to the tops of opposite sideposts; and (3) the lengthwise members, consisting

Fig. 3-2. Joined glass-covered greenhouses.

Fig. 3-3. Joined greenhouses that have double plastic-film roofs.

of the *eaves* at the juncture of the sidewall and the roof, the *ridge* at roof center, and the *purlins,* spaced equidistantly between the ridge and the eaves.

Covering.—The choice of a greenhouse covering is based on (1) sunlight transmission, (2) installation cost, (3) durability, (4) thermal insulation, and (5) flammability. Of these characteristics, the one that is of importance to plant growth is sunlight transmission. All of these characteristics are of economic interest.

There are continuous changes in the types of glass and plastics that may be used for greenhouse coverings. Before making the choice, greenhouse operators should get current information from greenhouse builders and examine various installations.

Size and Dimensions

Greenhouses are built in units called *bays.* The number of bays constructed determines the length. If the bays are 10 feet long and 11 bays are constructed, the greenhouse is 110 feet long.

The width is set for each type of greenhouse. If the greenhouse is 32 feet wide and has 10-foot bays, when 11 bays are used, the ground area covered is 32 feet by 110 feet, or 3,520 square feet.

The height of a greenhouse may be an option. For example, the 32-foot-wide greenhouse may be built with either 7- or 10-foot sidewalls.

Greenhouses may be built as either individual or joined units. If greenhouses are built as individual units there are sideposts and sidewalls on each side. If three 32-foot by 110-foot greenhouses are built so they are joined at the sides, adjoining roofs are connected to a *gutter* that is supported by the gutterposts. The area enclosed by these three joined greenhouses is 3 times 3,520 square feet, or 10,560 square feet.

Crop and equipment requirements.—The width and height of a greenhouse may need to be selected to suit the type of crop. For example, a 32-foot-wide greenhouse may be suitable for the total width of the benches and walks needed for pot-plant crops but may not fit the total width of the benches and walks needed for cut-flower crops. There may

Fig. 3-4. Greenhouse range with 6-foot benches for pot-plant production.

also be different requirements for greenhouse height, depending on crops and equipment.

Generally, rose flower crops require more height than pot-plant crops. However, when hanging-pot crops are grown above pot plants, the same greenhouse height may be required as with a cut-flower greenhouse. Greenhouse height must also provide space for overhead installations like heating pipelines, water pipelines, photoperiod lighting and covers, heaters, thermal insulation, high-intensity lighting, and sunlight screening.

Better crops can be grown when the bed or bench or the greenhouse size is crop-size because the entire crop usually requires the same work and adjustment of surroundings.

Beds and benches.—Greenhouse growing areas are generally called *beds* when the plants are in or on the ground and *benches* when the growing areas are constructed above the ground. The bed or bench width for cut-flower crops is usually either 3½ feet or 4 feet. The bench width for pot-plant crops is usually either 5 feet or 6 feet. Bed and bench lengths often are crop-length long, and that may be about 100

Fig. 3-5. Expanded metal bench for pot-plant production.

Fig. 3-6. Wooden bench for cut-flower production.

Fig. 3-7. Concrete ground bench for cut-flower production. The support network is at ground level for planting and will be raised as the chrysanthemum plants grow. The bench at right is covered in preparation for steaming.

Fig. 3-8. Support networks in a rose flower production range.

feet for cut-flower crops and about 50 feet for pot-plant crops.

The walks between growing areas generally are 1 ½ feet wide, and one walk in each area is wide enough for necessary equipment. In some pot-plant greenhouses, rolling bench tops are used so there is only one relocatable walk per five or six benches. There also are various methods of moving pot-plant benches into, around, and out of greenhouses during the cropping period. Some greenhouses do not have any walks between the benches, and access to the benches may be provided by catwalks above the plants.

Frequently bed, bench, and walk construction is handled by production and maintenance associates.

Cut-flower crops need support networks to maintain the upright growth of stems. The endposts for the support networks are part of bed or bench construction.

Sunlight

Greenhouses in the United States and Canada have to be con-

Fig. 3-9. Sunlight entry into a greenhouse through a glass-covered roof.

Fig. 3-10. Sunlight reflection from glass and plastic-covered greenhouse roofs. This greenhouse range was in flower and plant production for more than 60 years before the greenhouses were replaced.

structed so that sunlight (1) has free entrance from spring to fall; (2) can possibly be supplemented with high-intensity lighting from fall to spring; (3) can be shaded somewhat during summer; (4) can be supplemented by photoperiodic lighting as needed from fall to spring; (5) can be limited by photoperiodic shading as needed from spring to fall.

Free entrance.—Greenhouses cannot be completely transparent because of (1) blockage by framework and overhead equipment and (2) some transmission loss through coverings. Modern frameworks of various types admit comparable amounts of sunlight, but because of the shade from gutters, sunlight transmission usually is better in separate greenhouses than in joined greenhouses.

Greenhouse coverings vary mainly in sunlight transmission because of the (1) characteristics of the covering material and (2) amount of moisture that remains on the surface. The choice of a greenhouse covering is not a simple decision for greenhouse operators.

Supplemental-intensity lighting.—In the mid- and northern United States and in Canada, plant and flower production can be improved by supplemental-intensity lighting. However, before any lighting installation can be made, the possible net gain must be examined because of the cost of installation and operation. Also, lamp installation may be difficult in some greenhouses because of lack of greenhouse height or because of obstructions.

Shading.—Shading during the summer can improve plant growth by eliminating excessive light and heat. Movable shading is most suitable. If white thermal insulation is used in the winter, it may also be used for sunlight insulation in the summer.

Photoperiodic lighting.—Because of the widespread use of photoperiod control for chrysanthemum crops, photoperiodic lighting is sometimes known as mum lighting. Photoperiodic lighting is used for crops that need long photoperiods during the normally short fall-to-spring photoperiods. Sixty-watt incandescent lamps are spaced 4 feet apart and 2 feet above the plants. The lighting period is usually at about midnight and is controlled by timer.

Fig. 3-11. The movable cover in this rose range is used for sunlight shading from spring to fall and for heat insulation in cold weather.

**Fig. 3-12. Photoperiodic lighting
for chrysanthemum.**

Photoperiodic shading.—Photoperiodic shading must provide
light exclusion for plants. When the plants need to be in short photoperiods during the naturally long spring-to-fall photoperiods, black
plastic or fabric is placed around the crop plants each evening and
removed each morning.

Air

Generally, there is some exchange of air between outdoors and
indoors, which affects air qualities. With the exceptions of heat, water
vapor, and movement, outdoor air qualities remain quite uniform. In
the United States and Canada, outdoor air, as compared to indoor air,

Fig. 3-13. Manual photoperiodic shading for chrysanthemum.

Fig. 3-14. Automated photoperiodic shading that is also used for heat insulation in cold weather.

usually is cooler from fall to spring. Outdoor air temperatures during the summer may vary from cooler than to as hot as greenhouse temperatures. At night in any season, outdoor air temperatures are cooler than indoor air temperatures. Because of outdoor-indoor temperature differences, greenhouse air temperatures are reduced with the exchange of air.

Because air becomes drier with an increase in temperature, the indoor air usually becomes drier with the exchange with outdoor air. Although the effect on greenhouse air temperature may be the main reason for regulating air exchange, the accompanying change in air moisture also affects plant growth.

The exchange of air is regulated by the ventilation systems included in greenhouse buildings. If ventilation is not used regularly, the carbon dioxide in the indoor air may become low. Some greenhouse operators use carbon-dioxide generators or supply tanks for adding carbon dioxide to the air from fall to spring. Greenhouse ventilation may be provided by natural system or fan systems.

Natural ventilation.—Natural ventilation can occur because of the difference in weight between warm and cool air. The lighter warm air rises, and the heavier cool air descends, causing air circulation, or **convection currents.** If there are openings at greenhouse topside, warm air from indoors will exit and cool air from outdoors will enter. When a greenhouse is built, the roof may extend to within a few feet of the ridge, and the opening may be covered by a roof section hinged to the ridge. The hinged roof section, which can be opened or closed either manually or mechanically, is called a **ventilator.**

The operation of ventilators is usually based on temperature. If the indoor air is too warm, ventilators are opened so some warm air can be **vented** and then replaced with cool outdoor air. When ventilators are operated mechanically, they are regulated by **thermostats.**

In separate greenhouses, ventilators may also be hinged from the eaves so sections of the sidewall may be opened and closed.

Natural ventilation is more common with plane-surface greenhouses than with curved-surface greenhouses.

Fan ventilation.—**Exhaust fans** may be used to remove air from greenhouses. Usually exhaust fans are installed in one sidewall at regular intervals. There also must be openings in the greenhouse so air from outdoors will enter as the indoor air is exhausted by the fans. For cool-weather ventilation, shuttered openings are located at a high level in the endwall. A perforated, plastic-film tube with a closed end is attached to each opening. As indoor air is removed by the fans, outdoor air enters the wall opening and is distributed through the holes in the plastic-film tube. This type of ventilation system may be called *fan and tube.*

Fig. 3-15. Fan and tube ventilation. When shutters are open in endwalls and when exhaust fans in sidewalls are operating, air from outdoors is distributed through the plastic tubes inside the greenhouse roof.

For ventilation during hot weather, *fan and pad* cooling systems are used that consist of exhaust fans located in one sidewall, a pad installed in the opposite sidewall, and a water tank and distributor for moistening the pad.

During operation of the fan and pad system, the pad sidewall is opened and other greenhouse openings are closed so that when exhaust fans are operating, outdoor air can enter only through the moistened pad. Air passing through the pad causes evaporation of water and removal of heat from the entering air.

Heat

Sunlight is a main source of heat in greenhouses, but it is obvious that other heat sources are needed when sunlight is not available. It is

Fig. 3-16. Plastic-film ventilation tubes for air distribution in greenhouses.

possible that the heat from sunlight may be collected and stored for later use, but it is not probable that this process will be a source of heat in commercial greenhouses.

Fig. 3-17. These two greenhouses have fan and pad cooling systems. In the greenhouse at the left, the wall with pad and ventilator is in view. Exhaust fans are installed in the opposite wall of this greenhouse. In the greenhouse at right, the wall with exhaust fans is in view. The opposite wall of this greenhouse is enclosed with pad and wall ventilators.

Fuels are the main backup heating sources for greenhouses. Other sources of heat are (1) underground thermal water, (2) hot water circulated from electricity-generating plants, and (3) electric heating cables for propagating areas.

Generation.—Heat generation for steam and hot-water heating systems is usually located in adjacent buildings or **boiler rooms,** and the heat is transmitted by pipelines, or **mains,** as steam or hot water. The water and the condensed steam, or **condensate,** are returned to the boilers by pipelines called **return mains.** Boilers and mains may be installed either by greenhouse builders or by local contractors.

The operators of steam boilers usually have to be licensed.

Units to generate heat for hot air and infrared heating systems are located in the greenhouses.

Distribution.—Steam is distributed by continuous pipelines. The

Fig. 3-18. Pad for a fan and pad cooling system installed inside a greenhouse wall.

heating pipelines in greenhouses may be hung on benches, side- and endwalls, and trusses. In cold climates, one or more pipelines in joined houses are hung on gutterposts so snow can be melted to prevent damage to the greenhouses from the snow load.

Steam is also used for treating soil; separate pipelines are used for this purpose. This steam is exhausted into the soil.

Work with pipelines is called *pipefitting.* Production and maintenance associates usually do some of the pipefitting—either on heating or water pipelines. Heating pipelines are hung rather than firmly attached so they can move freely as they expand and contract with changes in temperature.

The temperature of steam-heating pipelines in greenhouses is about 220°F, but the temperature of the condensate that is returned to the boilers is 180°F or less. The temperatures of hot-water heating pipelines in greenhouses may vary from about 140° to 180°F.

Fig. 3-19. Steam boilers for heat generation.

The amount of heat supplied to greenhouses by steam and hot-water systems may be varied by the opening or closing of pipeline *valves.* Regulation of heating may be either manual, using hand valves, or mechanical, using electric valves, which are usually controlled by thermostatic operation.

Heat distribution by air heaters is provided by fans in the units, which are installed at uniform distances throughout greenhouses. Com-

Fig. 3-20. Steam-heating pipeline around a rose flower production bench. The pipeline starts at upper left and terminates at the steam trap at lower right.

Fig. 3-21. Steam-heating pipeline for a pot-plant bench.

Fig. 3-22. Overhead steam-heating pipelines are hung from the greenhouse framework.

Fig. 3-23. In joined greenhouses, steam-heating pipelines are hung from the gutter posts.

Fig. 3-24. Pipefitters' equipment. A pipe-thread cutter is at top. At bottom (left to right) are a pipe cutter, pipe dope, and pipe wrenches. At middle (left to right) are nipple, coupling, tee, union, elbow, cap, plug, and hand valve.

Fig. 3-25. Plastic tubelines for hot-water heating on a pot-plant bench.

monly, the air heaters dispense the heated air horizontally above the tops of the plants; some distribute heat by means of perforated tubes.

Usually, air heaters are electrically controlled by thermostats.

Infrared heating systems are continuous tubes with internal heat generators spaced at regular intervals. Overhead tubelines are spaced equidistantly with the ends of the tubelines exhausting combustion gases outdoors. Reflectors are installed above the tubelines. Heat from the infrared rays is distributed by the tubelines and reflectors to solid objects in the paths of the rays.

Heating is controlled by thermostats.

Fig. 3-26. Hot-air generator and plastic-film heat distribution tube.

Thermal insulation.—Because of the need for transparency, greenhouse buildings cannot have conventional thermal insulation but may have a special type of insulation. Some greenhouse operators use conventional thermal insulation on lower walls and north walls.

The greenhouse roof is the largest area for heat loss, and possible insulation there may be either double-layer covering or movable fabric.

Water

There must be good water supplies for greenhouse businesses. If municipal water is available, the quality and quantity of the water may be suitable, but the cost may be a major expense.

Own-source water may be pumped from ponds or wells, but the water quality and quantity must be verified.

Much of the water that is used in greenhouses is returned to the earth and must be satisfactorily removed from the greenhouse area.

Distribution. — Much of the water in greenhouses is dispensed with ¾-inch water hoses, and usually ¾-inch pipelines are installed so any location in the greenhouse can be reached by a 50-foot hose. Irrigation systems may require 1-inch pipelines or larger. These pipelines may be installed instead of or in addition to the ¾-inch pipelines.

Either plastic or galvanized steel pipe may be used for water pipelines. Production and maintenance associates usually do much of the installing.

Removal. — Greenhouse soil must have good drainage. Water must readily drain through container, bench, and bed soils and away from the greenhouse location.

Agricultural tile or plastic drain pipe is installed in the earth to improve the drainage in and around greenhouses. The flow from the tile and drain pipe is into streams, ponds, or large tile.

CONVENTIONAL BUILDINGS

Conventional buildings built by local contractors are the type that are used by various businesses for sales, accounting, warehousing, garage, and other purposes.

Light. — There is very little need for sunlight in conventional business buildings. Operators of retail flower shops may add some type of greenhouse to their shops, but these greenhouses are more for advertising and display than for growing. Display-type greenhouses usually are so heavily shaded that sunlight is almost excluded. Frequently,

Fig. 3-27. Hand-valve operation of a pot-plant irrigation system.

Fig. 3-28. Electric-valve operation of an irrigation system.

Fig. 3-29. Pot drainage.

Fig. 3-30. Wooden bench drainage.

conventional buildings do not have windows, or the windows are high enough so the wall areas can be used for business purposes.

The amount of lighting in conventional buildings is determined by the type of activity. Accounting and sales areas are well lighted, but buildings used for warehouse, garage, and potting may be minimally lighted.

Propagating areas in conventional buildings need excellent lighting.

Air.—There may be only a minimum exchange of air between outdoors and indoors in conventional buildings. There may be good air circulation, but generally this is continuous air circulation of indoor air, caused by heating and cooling systems.

Heat.—Conventional buildings used for accounting, sales, and offices have home-type heating and cooling systems and are regulated mainly for the comfort of the human occupants. The buildings used for warehouse, potting, and garage may have minimum heating and no cooling.

Moisture.—Generally, conventional buildings have dry interiors, and they may even be too dry in cold weather. Some conventional buildings used in floriculture businesses, like wholesale stores and potting buildings, must have provisions for the use and disposal of water.

Multilevel.—Because of the need for sunlight, greenhouses have to be one-level buildings. Some other business activities, however, can be above ground level. Accounting, offices, and living quarters may be on the second level or higher. Potting rooms or soil-storage buildings may have an elevated storage level. Buildings used for warehousing may be single-level but all racked.

EQUIPMENT

Emergency electricity generators.—The emergency electricity generator is needed for use during power outages. The generator must be large enough to ensure the operation of essential equipment like

(1) heating, (2) pumping, (3) ventilating and cooling, (4) refrigerating, and (5) basic lighting.

Soil handling and mixing.—Soil-handling and soil-mixing equipment varies with the type of crop and the size of operation. Some equipment may be purchased from local agricultural suppliers, but other items are available only through vendors of greenhouse equipment.

Transportation.—Motor vehicles used for delivery and sales routes may be purchased or leased.

Transportation equipment for use on the property may consist of manual carts, motorized carts, and various types of conveyors and trolley systems. Some are locally available; other types may be available only from vendors of greenhouse equipment.

Refrigeration.—Large refrigerators are needed for (1) storage of cut flowers during marketing, (2) cold treatment of bulbs in the fall, (3) cold treatment of budded azalea and hydrangea in the fall, and (4) storage of mature flowering plants during marketing.

Irrigation.—The minimum equipment required for irrigation is ¾-inch water hose. Good-quality hose is needed. It may be available from local industrial vendors.

The nozzles, tubes, mats, strainers, electric water valves, and timers needed for irrigation systems may be purchased from floriculture suppliers.

Fertilizer proportioners.—Fertilizer is applied mainly by the addition of dissolved fertilizer to irrigation water. Proportioners are available from floriculture vendors.

Pest and pathogen control.—Greenhouse operators need pest and pathogen control equipment, but the type depends on the form of the pesticides. The use of agricultural materials is guided by federal, state, or province regulations. Equipment needs are usually included in use instructions.

Bookkeeping and accounting.—Bookkeeping and accounting equipment usually is electronic and the type used by other businesses.

Fig. 3-31. Tube irrigation system for pot plants.

Fig. 3-32. Cut-flower irrigation system with pipe and nozzles installed at the bench side.

Fig. 3-33. Cut-flower irrigation system with pipe and nozzle installed at the center of the bed.

Machine shops.—Greenhouse businesses generally do much of their own maintenance and minor construction work. The machine shop may have a pipe cutter, a pipe threader, a drill press, and a general assortment of hand tools.

Misting and fogging.—If propagation is included in the business' operations, some misting-fogging equipment will be used. Nozzles, strainers, and electric water valves may be purchased from floriculture vendors.

Plant-surroundings control.—The three types of plant-surroundings control are (1) manual, (2) mechanical, and (3) electronic. The required equipment varies with the types of control. One or more of these types of control may be used in plant and flower production.

Thermometers are about the only kind of equipment used in manual control. For example, a grower observes the thermometer and manually adjusts heating and ventilating as needed. Some manual adjustment in heating and ventilating may be done in anticipation of daily or seasonal climate variations. Other manual operations may include irrigating the soil when it appears to be moist but somewhat dry, misting cuttings when the leaf surfaces appear to be dry, and opening the

**Fig. 3-34. Tube irrigation system
for cut-flower crops.**

carbon-dioxide supply valve from early morning to midafternoon when
there is no ventilation on days from fall to spring.

When systems and electricity are added, ventilating, heating, and
cooling can be operated by thermostats and motors, and irrigating and
misting can be controlled by timers and electric water valves. If there
are several units to be irrigated or misted in an area, timers can be
used to cause operation of the units in rotation. Also, if an electric
valve is installed in carbon-dioxide pipelines, that operation can be
controlled by a timer. In these operations, however, the only sensing
device used is a thermostat which can provide some automation of
ventilating, heating, and cooling. With misting and carbon-dioxide additions, the operation is controlled by preset timers. With an irrigation
operation controlled by timer, the timer for units to be irrigated is

Fig. 3-35. Tube and mat irrigation system for pot plants.

usually set and activated by the grower. Each unit to be irrigated then receives in rotation the same length of irrigation.

If electronic (computer) control and various types of sensors are added, it is possible that the operation of equipment for the control of plant surroundings may be automated and integrated. The equipment for this type of automation is expensive, and the success of the system depends on the reliability of the sensors and computer software that is used.

Chapter 4

ADJUSTING PLANT SURROUNDINGS

The plant surroundings that are generally adjusted are light, heat, air movement, moisture, and minerals. With the exception of sunlight, plant surroundings can be adjusted satisfactorily. Sunlight is adjusted as well as it can be, and then adjustments of other surroundings are based on that amount of light. Adjustments may vary with the kinds of plants and the stages of growth. The stages of growth may be called *propagation, early, active,* and *mature.*

STAGES OF GROWTH

Propagation.—General conditions for the propagation stage are low amount of light, warm bottom temperature, low soil minerals, moist air, and slight air movement. The propagation period is from several days to a few weeks, depending on the kind of propagation.

Early.—The early stage is a period of several days requiring a modest amount of light and proper photoperiod, warm bottom temperatures, some soil minerals, moist air, and moderate air movement.

Active.—The active stage is a period of active growth of stem, leaves, and roots, with full amount of light and proper photoperiod, correct day and night temperatures for specific kinds of plants, adequate soil moisture and minerals, and continuous air movement.

Mature.—Adjustments for the mature stage vary with the kind of plant, but generally the requirements are full amount of light and proper photoperiod, day and night temperature varied with flower development, somewhat limited soil moisture and minerals, and continuous air movement.

LIGHT

The amount of sunlight sets in action the other adjustments of plant surroundings because the amount of sunlight directly relates to the amount of heat. The greater the amount of sunlight entering greenhouses, the more heat there will be in and around plants.

Because of the varying relationships of the earth to the sun during the year, the amount of sunlight varies accordingly. In the United States and Canada, on about March 21 and September 21, day and night are of equal length, and the sun seems to be somewhat south of directly overhead at noon. On about December 21, the day length is the shortest of the year, and at noon the sun appears to be far to the south. On about June 21, the day length is the longest of the year, and at noon the sun seems to be directly overhead.

Because the amount of sunlight varies with the time of the day, the season of the year, and the clearness of the sky, adjustments of sunlight—and other surroundings—are affected by those events.

Time of day.—The daily sunlight intensity varies from zero before sunrise to maximum about noon, and then back to zero after sunset. The heat caused by sunlight follows that same sequence.

If the duration of sunlight is not correct for some crops, the photoperiod may need to be either lengthened by electric lighting or shortened by light-exclusion shading.

Because of the changes from sunlight to darkness and back to sunlight, the source of greenhouse heat from afternoon to morning has to be from a heating system.

Winter.—During the winter, the sunlight intensity is low and the daylength is short, creating less heat in greenhouses from sunlight. Any obstructions to sunlight should be removed early enough in the fall. Greenhouse coverings can be cleaned inside and outside, and hanging baskets and shelving can be removed.

Cultivars suitable for winter conditions should be used, and the plants may be spaced further apart to reduce shading among them.

If it is economically possible, high-intensity lighting may be installed.

The long photoperiods needed for some crops are provided by electric lighting.

Summer.—Sunlight during the summer may be too intense, causing excessively high temperatures in greenhouses. Shading of sunlight is generally used. Temperatures are reduced but still may be too high.

Cultivars suited for summer conditions should be used, and plants may be spaced closer together.

The short photoperiods needed for some crops are provided by daily exclusion of light with black fabric or plastic. Because the light exclusion has to be done during daylight, there may be excessive increases in temperatures under the covers. Since 12 hours are usually used for short photoperiods, covers could be placed at 7 p.m. and withdrawn at 7 a.m. However when the covers are handled manually, that timing would require an after-hours crew.

Growers who have the regular-hour associates handle the covers risk plant damage from high temperatures because the covers are placed before 5 p.m. daylight time, which actually is 4 p.m. standard time.

If short-photoperiod treatment is automated, the covers could be drawn at 7 p.m., withdrawn at about 11 p.m., drawn at about 3 a.m., and withdrawn at 7 a.m. Such a 12-hour photoperiod has the minimum amount of temperature increase.

Spring and fall.—Spring and fall sunlight conditions can be ideal. The problems that cause adjustments are variable weather conditions, mainly in the late spring and early fall. There may be day-to-day changes in sunlight intensity ranging from almost winter to summer conditions in the spring and from summer to winter conditions in the fall. This causes correspondingly variable heat conditions in the greenhouse.

The periods of variable sunlight can be adjusted when greenhouses are equipped with movable shading.

HEAT

Because sunlight changes to heat when it contacts plants, soil, and other solid objects in greenhouses, heat from heating systems has to be coordinated with the amount of sunlight. Greenhouses may be totally heated by sunlight, or they may have to be totally heated by heating systems when there is no sunlight.

The amount of heat needed depends on outdoor conditions—outdoor temperatures, clear or overcast skies, and amount of wind. Growers must have a good weather-forecasting service so heating and ventilating

Fig. 4-1. Thermometer at plant level in a carnation greenhouse.

Fig. 4-2. Thermostats for control of ventilation and heat in a mum greenhouse.

plans can be made at least 12 hours in advance. It is especially important to have warning of the arrival time of cold fronts and storms. Ice storms may injure greenhouse coverings and may cause electric-power outages. Heavy, wet snows may collapse greenhouses if there is not enough top heat to melt the snow as it falls. Double, plastic-film roofs may have to be deflated to allow rapid melting of snow.

On some days, there is too much heat, and it must be removed if possible.

Satisfactory growth of plants is possible only within very specific temperatures. It is possible to maintain those temperatures in greenhouses by suitable adjustments of sunlight, heating systems, ventilating and cooling systems, and refrigerating systems.

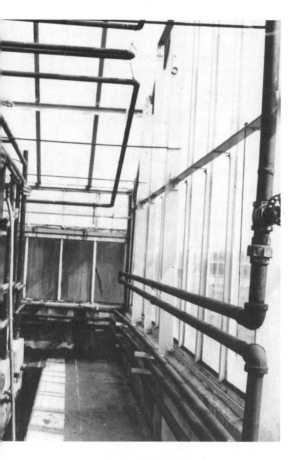

**Fig. 4-3. Hand valve for control
of steam-heating pipelines.**

Heat is sometimes adjusted because of the direct effects that it has on moisture. Generally, an increase in heat causes increases in evaporation and transpiration, a decrease in humidity, and dryer plant surfaces. An increase in heat usually causes an increase in air movement.

Time of day.—The daily schedule of sunlight-on and sunlight-off can be depended on. Heat from the heating system has to be as regularly scheduled so heat will be available before sunset until heat from sunshine is sufficient (sometime after sunrise).

Winter.—The need for daytime heating varies with the outdoor temperature and the clearness of the sky. When the skies are clear, sunlight may be the sole source of heat even in cold weather, and excess heat may be exhausted by ventilation.

On partly cloudy days, it is a real contest to provide heating and ventilating so greenhouse air temperatures remain constant as the sky switches from clear to cloudy to clear and back. Sometimes the solution is to operate the heating system uniformly and then to vent excess heat in the brief periods when sunlight reappears.

On overcast days, the main heat source may be the heating system, and there may be little change in the amount of heat from the sky throughout the day.

If overcast days are continuous, the effects of the lack of sunlight for plants can be modified by maintaining somewhat lower temperatures both day and night. In greenhouses equipped with high-intensity lighting, normal temperatures may be maintained during dark-weather periods.

At night, the heating systems are the sole sources of heat in greenhouses. The need for heat usually is more uniform at night than during the day, unless there are sudden temperature changes that occur with the arrival of cold fronts.

Because of greater heat loss from greenhouses on clear, windy nights, a greater amount of heat is needed than on overcast, still nights.

In any kind of weather, there is less heat loss from greenhouses equipped with thermal insulation.

Summer. — It would seem that there is no need for heating systems in United States and Canadian greenhouses during the summer, but greenhouses in some areas require some heat at night year-round and in other areas, for several nights during the summer.

The general greenhouse need in daytime is for heat removal. Also, there is need for heat removal at night in some greenhouses for several days to a few weeks. Maximum ventilation may be used day and night. General temperature limits are from 60° to 80°F. In daytime, there usually is no problem with the lower limit, but temperatures can easily exceed 80°F unless sunlight is shaded and fan and pad cooling is used from midmorning to midafternoon. Ventilation usually is continued after midafternoon, but water to pads is discontinued to prevent excess nighttime air moisture.

Spring and fall.—About the only thing certain about spring and fall outdoor temperatures is the trend. In the spring, the outdoor temperature trend is from cold to hot, and in the fall, the trend is from hot to cold. Usually there is not a uniform change in outdoor temperature each day. There are unpredictable temperature changes back and forth. Adjustment of greenhouse heating has to be just as flexible.

To be able to make needed adjustments, all systems affecting greenhouse temperature have to be available for use—heating, sunlight-shading, ventilating, and cooling.

AIR MOVEMENT

If there are openings in greenhouses, there is air movement that includes the exchange of indoor and outdoor air. Usually this is called ventilation. When greenhouses are closed, air movement within is usually called air circulation.

Air Exchange

When greenhouses are ventilated, it usually is for reducing either air temperature or air moisture. Another important result of the air exchange, however, is the replenishment of carbon dioxide and oxygen in the greenhouse air mixture.

Air temperature and moisture.—Frequently greenhouse ventilation is based only on the need for temperature adjustment. Thermometers are observed, and if temperatures are too high, ventilators are opened or fans are activated. When temperatures are too low, ventilators are closed or fans are stopped. If the ventilation system is automated, ventilator or fan operation is controlled by thermostats.

Whenever ventilation is operated, greenhouse air moisture as well as air temperature is affected. Ventilation for adjustment of air moisture could be by reference to psychrometers or each day at a set time in reference to the end-of-day change from sunlight heating to heating-system heating.

Other properties of air are affected during ventilation. The one of most consequence is in the amount of carbon dioxide in greenhouse air.

Carbon dioxide.—During cold weather, if there is no venting because temperature adjustment is not required, greenhouse air lacks enough carbon dioxide for photosynthesis. To prevent shortages of carbon dioxide, ventilation may be set for a period before noon for the adjustment of the carbon-dioxide level.

Because the growth or yield of some crops improves with higher than normal quantities of carbon dioxide, some greenhouses have carbon dioxide generators or tanks to increase the level to 1,000 parts per million (ppm) or more whenever possible from fall to spring. When carbon dioxide is added, ventilation is limited to necessary temperature and air-moisture adjustments.

Air Circulation

During ventilation there is air circulation within greenhouses. There also is air circulation in closed greenhouses when there is heating by sunlight or heating systems. At other times, in closed greenhouses there may be very little air circulation.

Fans may be installed in greenhouses to provide continuous air circulation. This mixing of air causes uniform quantities of heat, moisture, and carbon dioxide throughout the greenhouse air. Air circulation fans are usually operated whenever there is no ventilation.

MOISTURE

There is a constant need to adjust the amount of moisture in greenhouse soil and air. Soil moisture is increased by irrigation. Air moisture is increased by transpiration from plants and evaporation of water from irrigation or of other water used to spray, mist, and fog.

Air moisture is commonly increased to reduce water loss by transpiration in cuttings and young plants. In hot weather, air moisture may also be increased for mature plants.

Soil moisture needs to be replenished often enough so soils remain moist.

Air moisture may need to be decreased to prevent the growth of pathogens. Heating while ventilating is effective for decreasing air mois-

Fig. 4-4. For hose-in-hand irrigation of cut-flower crops, the fingers should be extended under the stream of water to cause a fan-shaped, less forceful flow of water.

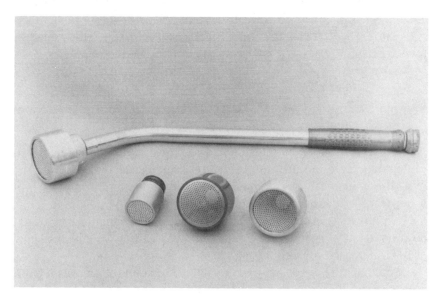

Fig. 4-5. Several types of water breakers may be used in hose-in-hand irrigation.

Fig. 4-6. Some hoze nozzles produce mist that is suitable for use on small plants like seedlings.

ture. Water loss from soils may be faster with bottom heating and air circulation.

Time of day.—Irrigation is usually started the first thing in the morning and completed by noon because (1) early irrigation prevents excessive drying due to an increase in sunlight, (2) soils dry rapidly and soil air increases, and (3) increased air moisture will vent before dark.

Misting and fogging to increase air moisture may be done from midmorning to midafternoon. That is the period when transpiration may be excessive and that scheduling allows enough time for plant surfaces to dry before sunset. A nighttime reduction of air moisture results from heating while ventilating from before until after sunset.

Winter.—Irrigations during the winter need to be as thorough as at any other time but have to be spaced further apart because water loss from soils is slower in the winter. If there is a question about the need for irrigation, a delay for another day is helpful during this time

Fig. 4-7. For hose-in-hand irrigation of pot plants, a low rate of water flow is used, and water delivery is pot-by-pot.

of the year. The use of bottom heating and constant air circulation may help speed water loss by evaporation.

In propagation and for young plants, there may be a need for an increase in air moisture because of moisture loss to the inside of greenhouse coverings in cold weather. This need for adjustment may be greater at night than during the day. For disease control of mature crops, heating while ventilating is effective for drying plant surfaces.

Summer.—Irrigations need to be thorough and frequent because soils dry rapidly with increased sunlight and heat. If there is a question about the need for irrigation, it is usually best to irrigate today rather than tomorrow.

Because of the increased transpiration associated with excessive sunlight and heat, air moisture should be increased by misting or fogging.

Spring and fall.—It is difficult to know what the weather will be tomorrow or next week. Constant reference to weather forecasting can be helpful. Irrigate today if the forecast is good, and delay for a day when the forecast is for overcast and cool.

Fig. 4-8. Tube-to-pot irrigation methods allow automation of irrigation.

Fig. 4-9. Continuous inspection for wilted plants is needed to locate plugged or missing tubes.

Fig. 4-10. Automated irrigation of a cut-flower crop, with pipelines and nozzles installed at bench sides.

MINERALS

Adjustment of minerals varies with the kind of soil. Mineral soils (formed from rocks) require less adjustment than organic soils (peat moss) or soil mixtures that do not contain mineral soils.

Minerals are used in the form of mineral compounds or mixtures of mineral compounds called *fertilizers.* They may affect soil acidity-alkalinity (pH) in addition to increasing the mineral supply.

Some minerals are added when soils are mixed in preparation for planting. Other minerals are supplied regularly during the cropping period. In the case of mineral soils, fertilizers containing compounds of calcium, phosphorus, magnesium, and chemicals for pH adjustment are usually mixed with the soils before planting, and no further adjust-ment with those materials may be needed during the cropping period.

During crop production, the dissolved fertilizer added to irrigation water contains compounds of nitrogen, potassium, and possibly some chemicals for pH adjustment. The nitrogen compounds may be both nitrate and ammonium forms of nitrogen. During the winter, mainly the nitrate form of nitrogen is used.

There are many variations in soil mixtures that do not contain mineral soils. Vendors of these soil mixtures must specify the kinds and amounts of fertilizers to be used before and after planting.

Chapter 5

WORKING WITH PLANTS

Direct work with plants may involve propagating; planting; pinching; using manufactured growth regulators; disbudding and pruning; spacing; harvesting; moving; and controlling pests, weeds, and pathogens. This work is effective only if it is carefully timed.

PROPAGATING

In all types of propagating, plant materials are placed in surroundings that favor the development of roots. With some types of plant material, the surroundings also have to be suitable for the development of shoots. In all types of propagating, the plant materials and surroundings have to be free of pathogens.

Various types of plant materials may be used in propagating. Through the years the common plant materials used for propagating have been seed, stem-tip and stem-segment cuttings, leaves, and segments of leaves and roots. More recently, propagating has included laboratory procedures that use very small sections of plant material.

The main sources of plant material for propagating are specialist producers. Seed comes from breeders who produce either inbred seed or F_1 hybrid seed. Stem and leaf propagating materials come from specialists who maintain stock-plant supplies. These specialists often develop new cultivars either by hybridization or by selection of mutants.

They also have laboratories for culture-indexing to ensure that pathogen-free stock is maintained. They are producers of crop-starter plants that may be used for either stock plants or crop-producing plants.

The discussions here deal with some of the crops that may be propagated by plant and flower producers.

Surroundings

Propagating may be done in greenhouses or general-purpose buildings, providing the following surroundings can be maintained.

Light.—The light source may be either sunlight or electric lighting, or it may be a combination of these two sources. If the light source is sunlight, enough shade has to be used so the maximum light intensity is about 500 foot-candles until the start of root development. The amount of light can then be increased gradually during the propagation period.

If the light source is electric lighting, fluorescent lamps are usually used, operated by timer for 16-hour photoperiods.

Heat.—Bottom heat is required, and it must provide uniform soil temperature. The soil temperature needed for the propagation of most types of plants is 70°F. Propagating areas usually need separate heating systems either because the heating systems for greenhouses cannot supply bottom heat or because the heat supply is not continuous. Electric cables or hot-water boilers may be used as heat sources for propagating areas.

Air temperature is usually maintained at 60°F, both day and night.

Moisture.—Mist systems are used to provide the frequent but brief mistings required to keep seed or cuttings moist during rooting. When roots start to form, the frequency of misting is decreased gradually.

After the seed is sown or the cuttings are stuck, the soil is thoroughly irrigated. Although the misting system is operated so there is no addition of moisture to the soil, the soil may not have to be irrigated again until after the roots develop.

Air movement.—There may be enough air movement in propagating areas because of convection currents caused by bottom heating.

Fig. 5-1. Chrysanthemum propagation by stem-tip cuttings. A misting pipeline is installed above the bench.

Fig. 5-2. Chrysanthemum propagation by stem-tip cuttings. Misting is in operation.

Unless barriers are installed, there usually is too much air movement when propagating is done in part of a production greenhouse. Excessive air movement causes drying of plant material as well as uneven distribution of mist.

Soils and containers.—Soils used in propagation may vary in many characteristics, but regardless of the differences, each type of soil must have the following qualities: (1) pathogen free, (2) easily wetted and free drainage, (3) suitable pH—generally pH 6.5, and (4) low quantities of fertilizer compounds and soluble salts.

Various types of containers are used, and the soil must be suitable for use with the container. Sometimes the soil also is the container, like compressed peat moss or foam materials. Generally, propagating soils have uniformly small particles so there is good contact with seed, stem, or roots.

Commonly used containers include benches, flats, pots, packs, and plug trays.

The depth of planting in propagating soil varies with the plant material. Tiny seed is usually sown on the soil surface and is not covered. Large seed is covered with soil. The grower should refer to seed catalogs for specific directions for sowing each kind of seed.

Cuttings are generally stuck as shallowly as possible.

Plant Materials

The plant materials used in propagation are either seed or some vegetative parts of plants like stems and leaves. Greenhouse growers seldom produce seed for starting their crops. The seed they use may originate with plant breeders in several locations in the world.

Greenhouse growers may use some of their crop plants as sources of plant material for propagation. This is fairly common practice with African violet and with some of the foliage plants. Usually growers set aside some plants for use only as stock plants.

Seed.—Plant breeders produce seed by self-pollination (inbreeding) and cross-pollination (crossbreeding). Some of the inbred seed is used directly for starting greenhouse crops. Other self-pollination work produces inbred seed for the production of pure-line plants for use in cross-pollination in the production of F_1 hybrid seed.

Plant-breeding work, as well as extensive trialing, may be done in either greenhouses or fields.

Stems and leaves.—Greenhouse growers may use crop-starter plants produced by specialty propagators either directly for starting plant- and flower-production crops or for starting stock plants that produce stems for the growers' own propagation of crop-starter plants. Several growers start stock plants to produce their own propagating plant material for poinsettia and geranium crops. Some chrysanthemum growers also produce their propagating material in this way. The specialty propagators may charge the growers a royalty for each cutting propagated from the stock plants.

Garden Plants

Most garden plants are propagated by seed. The times for sowing and propagating vary with the cultivars, and seed-vendors' catalogs provide the specific information that is needed. Some of the most important garden-plant crops are ageratum, alyssum, begonia, cabbage, geranium, impatiens, marigold, petunia, salvia, and tomato.

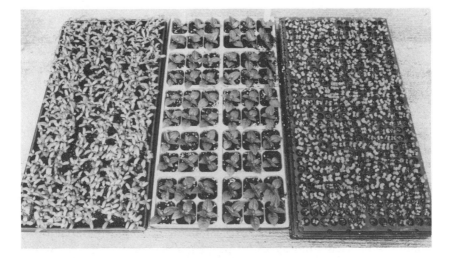

Fig. 5-3. Propagation methods for some garden crops. From left to right: seed sown in rows; cuttings stuck in packs; and seed sown in plug tray.

Fig. 5-4. Geranium stock plants.

Geranium

Geranium is propagated by stem-tip cuttings as well as by seed. The geranium propagated by seed may be marketed in various sizes of containers, from packs to 4-inch pots. Geranium propagated by cuttings are usually marketed in 4-inch pots. Because of their susceptibility to serious diseases, stock plants are usually started with pathogen-free plants purchased from specialty propagators. Because the geranium market is in the spring, the stock plants are started from summer to fall, depending on the month the plants will be marketed. The stock plants are grown in 7- or 8-inch pots; some of the stock plants may be grown for sale as large flowering plants. Each stock plant may be allowed to produce one flower to verify that the correct cultivar will be propagated, but further flower buds are removed during cutting production. A plant-growth regulator that increases branching may be applied to the stock plants.

Stem-tip cuttings are harvested about three months before the first pot-plant marketing period. Cutting harvest continues until about two months before the latest marketing period. To increase the yield of cuttings from stock plants, some geranium growers use stem-segment cuttings as well as stem-tip cuttings.

The cuttings are usually stuck directly into the 4-inch pots they will be grown in. The pots are placed pot-to-pot in benches that have bottom heat, and the plants are periodically misted until the roots start to develop. A uniform air temperature of 60°F is usually maintained.

Fig. 5-5. Geranium unrooted and rooted stem-tip cuttings.

Poinsettia

Poinsettia pot-plant producers often propagate the stem-tip cuttings needed to start their crops. The marketing period for the mature plants is from November to December, and the rooted cuttings are needed during July to September.

The stock-plant crop is started from cuttings purchased from specialists who can supply pathogen-free plants. From April to June, the stock plants are planted in beds, benches, or pots. The greenhouse night temperature used is 70°F.

The stock plants require long photoperiods for stem and leaf growth. Early plantings should be provided with electric lighting each night. Some growers use electric lighting during the entire propagating period so they are sure that the photoperiods are long and that stem and leaf growth is continuous.

The stock plants are pinched to cause branching and to increase the yield of cuttings. The pinch is made above three fully expanded leaves. Succeeding pinches or cutting harvest may be made at about four-week intervals. The plants are examined weekly, and necessary pinches are made. If the stems are allowed to grow too long before cuttings are made, flower formation may start, regardless of long photoperiods, and the cuttings made from these long stems may produce branched-flowering (splitting).

For the production of large plants, stem-tip cutting harvest is started in July and then is continued at intervals up to September for the production of gradually smaller plants.

Poinsettia cuttings are generally stuck in small pots or packs. Some growers stick the cuttings in the pots in which they will be grown. The size of cutting usually is 3 to 4 inches.

African Violet

Leaf cuttings are used for propagating African violet. The source of the leaves usually is from stock plants maintained by the grower. The leaf is cut with about ½-inch of petiole and then stuck upright in a soil-filled flat so the leaf blade is at soil surface. The roots develop from the petioles, followed by shoot development. Several shoots form per leaf. At 70°F soil temperature, the new plant may be separated from the leaf in about 2½ months and then potted in packs or small pots.

Propagation usually is year-round for continuous plant production in 4-inch pots.

Fig. 5-6. African violet propagation by leaf cuttings.

Cyclamen

Cyclamen is propagated with seed. Because the seed is large, it is sown individually in soil-filled packs. The germination temperature is 70°F, followed by a seedling growth temperature of 60°F.

The time of sowing for fast cropping is March to April for plants to be marketed in 6½-inch pots December to February.

Cineraria

Cineraria is propagated with seed sown from late summer to fall for plants to be marketed in 6½-inch pots January to March. Cineraria seed is small and is usually sown in rows on the surface in soil-filled flats. At 70°F, germination occurs in about 10 days. The seedlings are grown at 60°F and then transplanted to packs or small pots.

Snapdragon

Snapdragon seedlings are transplanted directly to the crop-production bench about one month after the seed has been sown. Because the seed is small, it is sown on the soil surface in rows. At 70°F, the seed germinates in about 10 days. The seedlings are grown at 60°F.

PLANTING

Planting usually refers to the placing or setting of plants in soil; but actually, the preplanting and postplanting activities all are part of the planting procedure. The main preplanting activity is preparing the soil for planting. The postplanting activities are regulating moisture, light, and heat.

Potting is the term often used when the planting is being done in pots. The term *transplanting* is sometimes used when plants are being planted again, like transplanting snapdragon seedlings from seed flats to production benches or transplanting plants in small pots to larger pots.

Preparing Soil for Planting

Field or mineral soils without amendment generally are not suitable for use in greenhouses. When greenhouse soils are prepared for planting, materials are added to mineral soils to (1) improve drainage, (2) add needed fertilizers, and (3) adjust the soil pH. The soil and added materials are then cultivated or mixed so all materials are evenly distributed and particle size is nearly uniform. Greenhouse soils are usually steamed before planting to eliminate pests, pathogens, and weeds.

Pot-plant growers who base their soil mixtures on mineral soils usually use at least 15 percent mineral soil in the mixtures. Cut-flower growers may use about 80 percent mineral soil.

Some pot-plant growers do not use any mineral soils in their soil mixes. They either prepare their own mixtures or they purchase manufactured mixes. The composition of the manufactured mixes varies considerably, but the requirements for drainage, fertilizer, pH, and freedom from pests, pathogens, and weeds remain just the same as they do for mixtures which include mineral soil.

Improving drainage.—Plant materials like peat moss, chopped straw, and shredded bark are often used to improve soil drainage. Nonplant materials like haydite, perlite, and calcined clay are also used.

More drainage improvement is required with pot-plant soils because they are more shallow than cut-flower soils and drain more slowly than cut-flower soils.

Adding fertilizers.—The fertilizers commonly added to soils before planting are compounds of calcium, phosphorus, and magnesium. The type of fertilizer that is used may be varied because of its effect on the soil pH. For example, agricultural limestone is used for calcium supply when raising the soil pH is required, or gypsum is used for calcium supply when no adjustment of the soil pH is required.

Some fertilizers contain more than one kind of fertilizer material. Superphosphate is the fertilizer commonly used to supply phosphorus. Calcium is also supplied because this fertilizer is a calcium phosphate compound. Agricultural limestone is of two types—calcite and dolomite. Calcite is a calcium compound, and dolomite is a calcium-magnesium compound. Epsom salts is a fertilizer that is a magnesium compound.

Ferrous sulfate is a fertilizer that may be used if the soil pH needs to be adjusted downward. This fertilizer is an iron compound.

Mixing soil.—The way soil is mixed varies with the crop. In small batches, pot-plant soils may be mixed by manually turning the soil pile with a shovel. Some pot-plant growers mix larger batches with a tractor front-end shovel. There are various types of rotary mixers used for pot-plant soils. Each material is added independently to the pile or mixer, and during turning or mixing, the materials are uniformly distributed. Some of the rotary mixers include steaming along with the mixing process.

Cut-flower soils are cultivated in the beds or benches where they will be used. Cultivation may be done manually with a spade fork or by rotary cultivators. The drainage-improvement materials are usually distributed on the soil surface in terms of inches of material. Fertilizers needed per bed or bench are weighed and then uniformly distributed on the soil surface by hand. Uniformity of distribution is more likely if half-quantities are weighed and two applications are made.

Steaming.—Greenhouses with steam-heating systems have a source of steam for treating soil. Steam for treating soil may also be generated by some hot-water heating systems. Greenhouses with other types of heating systems may use either stationary or mobile steam generators just for the purpose of steaming soils.

Some chemical products can be used instead of steam for treating soil, but steaming usually is more effective.

If pot-plant soils are not steamed in the mixer, they are usually steamed in an enclosed container, chest, truck bed, or wagon.

Cut-flower soils are steamed in the beds or benches where the crops will be grown.

Steam heat transfers more readily through moist soils than it does through either dry or waterlogged soils. As the steam enters the soil, air is forced out. With potting soils, the steam is injected at a lower level, and the air is exhausted at the top surface of the soil. After the air is exhausted, the soil container is covered so the heat is retained in the soils.

With cut-flower soils, the steam distributor is usually placed on the soil surface and bed or bench is enclosed with a steam-proof cover. As steam enters the soil, the air exhausts through the bed or bench bottoms.

Steaming continues until all areas of the soil maintain a minimum temperature of 150°F for one-half hour. The cover is then removed, and the soil is allowed to cool.

When pot-plant soils are steamed in truck or wagon, potting may be done from the drop-side of the vehicle. When other means of steaming are used, the steamed soil is transported to the potting location.

Cut-flower soils have to be leveled after steaming so irrigation water can drain uniformly through the soil. If the soil surface is not level at the time of planting, there is no way it can be leveled satisfactorily after planting.

Plants and Area

The plants need to be at the correct stage of growth before planting. Seedlings should be planted as soon as they are large enough to be handled. Cuttings should be planted when their roots are about ½ inch long. Geranium and poinsettia are two types of cultivars that grow very well when they are planted as callused cuttings—before actual roots develop. Plants that are left in propagation until the seedlings are tall or until the cuttings are heavily rooted do not grow as satisfactorily as younger plants do.

Plants in packs and small pots also need to be planted as soon as possible. Their roots need to be grown enough so the soil ball is contained by the roots when the plants are knocked out of the pots. More root development than that can cause slower growth of the plant after planting. Plants that have a solid mass of mature roots encircling the soil ball develop new roots very slowly after planting.

The planting climate has to be satisfactory for the plants—only moderate light, temperature, and air movement—so the plants do not dry. Planting pot plants is usually done in potting rooms where the climate is easily controlled. Cut-flower planting is usually done in greenhouses, where the small plants being planted may be damaged by bright sunlight and high temperatures. The planting area should be shaded from sunlight. This is particularly important in planting small seedlings like snapdragon but is not of much concern in planting bulbs like iris.

Transportation needs to be well planned so there is continuous planting. With pot-plant crops, transportation is needed to and from the potting room. Plants to be potted may have to come from greenhouses, propagation areas, or receiving areas. The potted plants have to be labeled and transported to greenhouses. Pots must be in adequate supply. Labels should be prepared for placement in planted pots. The greenhouse area has to be ready for the newly potted plants, and the spacing of plants must be understood.

The transportation of cut-flower plants for greenhouse planting is not so involved, but it is necessary to arrange for enough plants to be available for planting to be continuous without much storage time in a hot greenhouse. Labels must be carefully read so correct cultivars can be planted together.

Before the start of planting, cut-flower planters have to know how many plants are to be planted across the bed or bench, how many rows of plants there are to be, and whether that quantity of plants is available. The entire bed or bench must be marked before planting so it can be determined that the required number of rows will fit and so it can be seen that the plants will be in straight rows and lines.

Planting

Generally, shallow planting is recommended because it causes faster root growth. There are also better chances that the stems and roots will remain healthy because the bottom stem tissues are more mature and less susceptible to disease. The soil must be moist at the time of planting, and the roots of seedlings and rooted cuttings should barely be covered with soil. Plants in pots are set in the new location at the same depth as they were in the original pot. The main kinds of planting are seedlings, rooted cuttings, small pot plants, bulbs, dormant plants, and larger pot plants.

Because the roots of any type of plant must be prevented from drying during planting, they should be exposed to the air for the shortest possible time before planting.

After planting a container, whether a pot or a bench, the soil surface must be lower than the top edge of the container so that, during irrigation, water can collect on the soil surface and drain uniformly through the soil.

Because seedlings are tiny and succulent, they must be handled gently. Seedlings are held by a leaf rather than by the stem. Firming the soil around the stem and roots must be done carefully. Seedlings awaiting planting have to be protected from drying. Moist toweling can be placed over exposed roots and stems. Because of the small size of the plants, a *dibble* is generally used instead of the fingers. A hole is made in the soil with the dibble, the roots are lowered into the hole, and the soil is backfilled and firmed with the dibble also.

Rooted cuttings are planted with the fingers. Soil is scooped aside with one hand, and the roots are lowered into the hole with the other hand. Soil is firmed around the roots and stem by a single downward movement of the thumbs and forefingers of both hands.

In small-pot planting, the plant is knocked out of the original pot and set in a larger pot that contains enough soil so that when potting is completed, the plant will be at the same level as it was in the original pot. After the plant is set in the pot, soil is filled around the soil ball, and the plant is set firmly in the soil with a single downward movement of the thumbs and forefingers of both hands.

Bulbs are generally planted so the tips of the bulbs extend just above the soil surface. Easter-lily bulbs are an exception. They are planted deeply.

Fig. 5-7. Planting mum stem-tip rooted cuttings.

Older bare-root plants may require root pruning before they are planted. For each plant, a sufficiently large hole is dug with a trowel, the roots are lowered into the hole, and soil is backfilled over the roots with the trowel.

A pot plant is repotted in a larger pot which contains enough soil so that the plant will be at the same level as it was in the original pot. Then, soil is filled between the pot and the soil ball. The plant is settled in the pot by tapping the pot bottom on the table.

Postplanting

After planting, the plants need to have surroundings that are suitable for prompt root growth. The soil is watered as soon as possible after planting to ensure good contact of the soil with the roots and stems. Pot plants must be moved promptly to the greenhouse so the soil can be watered. In hot weather, the soil for cut-flower plants can be watered as planting continues. This is better than waiting to water until the entire planting is complete. For about two weeks, the after-

Fig. 5-8. Rose plant two weeks after planting.

planting surroundings should include bottom heating; shading; and frequent, brief misting that keeps the stems and leaves moist but does not add water to the soil.

PINCHING

Pinching is the removal of stem tips. Greenhouse growers pinch plants either to cause branching or to change the time of flowering. Pinching also decreases the height of plants.

The terms *soft pinch* and *hard pinch* are sometimes used to describe the types of pinch. The soft pinch is made closer to the stem tip than the hard pinch. The definitions of these terms are not always clearly understood, and instructions are better if they are in reference to leaves—either to the number of leaves left on the stem or to the position of the first mature leaf from the stem tip. The term *pinch* describes the method often used in stem-tip removal. The stem tip is removed by squeezing the thumb and forefinger at the point where the stem is to be severed. Pinching more mature stems is accomplished with knife in hand.

Branching.—Some greenhouse plants are selfbranching—they have natural, bushlike growth, for example, cineraria, exacum, and begonia. Examples of greenhouse plants that do not have the selfbranching type of growth are carnation, chrysanthemum, and rose. Some greenhouse plants, like dieffenbachia, geranium, and poinsettia, have cultivars of each type—selfbranching and nonbranching.

If pinching is used to cause branching, it is done early in the growth of the plants. The instructions may be to leave a certain number of leaves on the stem. For example, the instruction may be "to pinch to" or "to leave" two leaves. The purpose may be to produce a bushy, short

Fig. 5-9. Chrysanthemum stem to be pinched.

Fig. 5-10. Pinching a chrysanthemum stem.

Fig. 5-11. Pinched chrysanthemum stem.

Fig. 5-12. Rose plant young stem to be pinched.

pot plant for marketing or a bushy plant for the production of a greater number of cuttings or flowers. Sometimes the shoots that develop from the pinch are also pinched to produce even more stems for cuttings or flowers. Pinching delays production but increases yield later.

Timing crops.—Pinching is commonly used to time rose crops for marketing periods. The pinches are made to allow time for the flowers to develop according to the season. For example, rose stems may be pinched about eight weeks before the Valentine's Day market or about six weeks before the Mother's Day market.

Improving stem quality.—Rose stems that are too short or too weak are pinched to improve stem length or sturdiness.

USING MANUFACTURED PLANT-GROWTH REGULATORS

The growth of greenhouse plants is continuously regulated by adjustments of light, heat, moisture, fertilizer, air, time of planting, pinching, pruning, disbudding, and harvesting. Further regulation of the growth of some kinds of plants can result from the use of manufactured products. Because of continuous changes in products and procedures, the specific information about them and their uses must be obtained from current publications and instructions.

Plant growth—regulating products may be used for their effects on rooting, height, branching, and flowering.

DISBUDDING AND PRUNING

Disbudding is the removal of some flower buds from the terminal flower stems of certain cultivars that have more than one flower bud per stem. If all the flowers were allowed to develop, there would be a cluster of flowers per stem. The terminal flower is the largest flower in each cluster, and it matures sooner than the lateral flowers.

If all of the lateral buds are removed, there will be a solitary large flower per stem.

If only the terminal flower bud is disbudded, there will be a cluster

Fig. 5-13. Standard (commercial) chrysanthemum stem to be disbudded.

Fig. 5-14. Disbudding a standard (commercial) chrysanthemum stem.

Fig. 5-15. Disbudded standard (commercial) chrysanthemum stem.

of smaller flowers per stem, with all of the flowers maturing more uniformly.

Disbudding is a common procedure with chrysanthemum, with carnation, and to some extent with rose.

Disbudding has to be done as soon as the flower buds are large enough to be handled without damage to the stem, leaves, and other flower buds. Usually the unwanted flower buds can be rolled or pinched by hand when disbudding is done promptly.

Pruning is the removal of some plant stems to improve the future growth or appearance of the plant. For example, chrysanthemum and snapdragon cut-flower crops can be grown either single-stem or pinched. With pinched crops, the length and sturdiness of the stems and the size of the flowers depend on the number of stems allowed to mature. If more than two shoots develop after pinching, the two sturdiest shoots may be allowed to grow, and the balance of the shoots may be pruned as soon as the shoots can be handled.

A different type of pruning is used with the rose. The stems are cut about 2 to 3 feet above the soil yearly because this type of pruning keeps the rose plants within working height for the growers.

Fig. 5-16. Spray chrysanthemum stem to be disbudded.

Fig. 5-17. Disbudding a spray chrysanthemum stem.

Fig. 5-18. Disbudded spray chrysanthemum stem.

Fig. 5-19. Greenhouse flats for moving plants.

SPACING, HARVESTING, AND MOVING

Spacing of pot plants and harvesting of cut flowers and pot plants cause movement of plants and flowers.

The spacing of cut-flower plants is done only at planting time. The plants are not moved again until cropping is finished and the plants are discarded. Many of the pot-plant crops are moved during the cropping period. After potting, the plants are moved from the potting area to the greenhouse area, where they may be set pot-to-pot for a few weeks before being moved to their final spacing. Four times more area may be required for final spacing, so the plants must be moved to other benches or possibly to other greenhouses.

The need for temperature changes may cause movement of pot plants. Some crops require cold temperatures before forcing, so the plants are first moved to refrigerators, where the plants are set pot-to-pot. Later the plants are moved to greenhouses for forcing.

All of the plants in a crop do not mature at the same time. Plants that are behind schedule may be moved to greenhouses that have warmer temperatures. Plants that are ahead of schedule may be moved to cooler greenhouses or to refrigerators. The remaining plants are regrouped to allow space for other plants.

Some plants are started in small pots and later repotted in larger pots. The moves then would be from the potting area to greenhouse with small-pot spacing. In a few weeks, the small pots would be moved back to the potting area to be shifted to larger pots, which then are returned to greenhouses, possibly at mature-plant spacing. This final spacing would require about nine times more greenhouse area than the plants in smaller pots used. If greenhouse area is scarce, the grower may decide to grow the plants in a smaller bench area for a few weeks and then to respace them to mature-plant spacing. Changes in the spacing of pot plants cause the moving of just about every pot in the crop.

Fig. 5-20. Rose flower maturity. Development of the flower at center is satisfactory for harvest.

The time of harvest of cut-flower crops is apparent because the flowers are harvested at a certain stage of maturity, and that signal for harvesting is usually rather obvious. Greenhouse flowers are usually cut with knife in hand, and the cut flowers are carried in the harvester's other arm. In some instances, flowers are also cut with shears. When the worker's arm is loaded, the cut flowers are placed in water-filled vases in the greenhouse's center walk. Usually the vase water is adjusted to pH 3.5 with citric acid. The harvesters may be required to register the quantity of flowers cut on a form in the greenhouse. While cutting the flowers, harvesters are able to make observations on the conditions of the plants and their surroundings. Typical observations that can be made are (1) what stems need to be replaced in the supporting network, (2) evidence of pests, (3) evidence of disease, (4) suitability of temperature, (5) suitability of soil moisture, (6) location of steam or water leaks, (7) suitability of ventilation, and (8) damage to greenhouse covering. Cut-flower harvesters get around the entire greenhouse daily, and their reports on general conditions are valuable to greenhouse operators.

As soon as possible, the harvested flowers are transported either to refrigerators or to the grading area. Cut flowers are graded and bunched either before or after refrigeration. The graders keep a record of the number of flowers that are processed. Cut-flower refrigerators are operated at 40° to 45°F, and vase water must be clean and treated with citric acid. The flowers are usually refrigerated overnight and then marketed.

The time of harvest is not so obvious with pot plants as it is with cut flowers. Harvest time of flowering pot plants can be based on flower maturity, but there are less obvious harvest signals with foliage plants, crop-starter plants, and garden plants. Greenhouse operators determine when to harvest these plants on the basis of various signs of plant maturity.

With most pot-plant crops, maturity varies among the plants in the crop. Depending on the operator and on the type of crop, any of four general methods of plant harvest may be used: (1) the mature plants may be selected daily and grouped in a market-ready area, (2) the majority of the plants may be marketed, and the balance retained for further growth, (3) the plants may be selected daily to fill orders, (4) the entire crop may be either sold or discarded. All of these harvesting methods require the movement of plants, and some plants will require double movement because of regrouping and later harvest.

Pot-plant harvesting includes cleaning of pots and removing plant

Fig. 5-21. Pot mums being sleeved for delivery.

defects. The plants are usually sleeved for shipment, and some are placed in cartons. Irrigation of pot plants must be carefully timed with the harvest. The soil must be moist when the customer receives the plant, yet the soil cannot be too wet for the marketing period.

PESTS, PATHOGENS, AND WEEDS

The feeding activities of pests and pathogens damage plants. Weeds may also cause plant damage because weeds may either host pests and pathogens that may transfer to crop plants or compete with crop plants for sunlight, water, and fertilizer.

Pests and Pest Damage

Plant pests are small, and many of them have wings. Insect pests reproduce mainly by eggs, and after the eggs hatch, growth proceeds by a series of molts *(metamorphosis)*. The young individuals may look and feed about the same as the adults (thrips, for example) or they may look and feed very differently from the adults. Fungus gnat and leafminer are examples. The adults are winged flies, and the young are crawling *larvae.*

Common pests that are not insects are mites, slugs, and garden symphylans.

Aphid.—Aphids are about BB-size and may be green, tan, or brown. They may or may not have wings. Aphids often cluster on stem tips.

Fig. 5-22. Aphids on cineraria.

Often, residues from aphids are very noticeable. Honeydew is syrupy and may be covered with black mold, and bits of tan or white skins may be cast on leaf surfaces.

Thrips.—Often thrips are not seen, but the results of their activities are obvious and characteristic. Thrips locate in stem tips—commonly in developing flowers. Their feeding activities are so great that tissues are killed and growth is malformed.

Thrips are winged and have the ability to soar long distances on wind currents.

Cyclamen mite.—Cyclamen mites are too tiny to be observed by eyesight, but the malformed growth caused by their feeding in plant tips is characteristic. African violet is a common host. In addition to the characteristic small, thick, malformed leaves, the leaf hairs of infested African violet are very dense and long.

Twospotted mite.—The twospotted mite is also called *red spider* and *spider mite.* These mites can be observed if eyesight is good. Twospotted mites generally locate on the undersurface of leaves. Their feeding causes speckling of the upper surface of leaves that is typical and noticeable.

When there are large numbers of mites in an infestation, they may produce webbing over the plants.

Whitefly.—Whiteflies are indeed white and leave in a flurry when they are disturbed from their underleaf locations.

Fig. 5-23. Twospotted mites on the rose leaf at right.

Fig. 5-24. Moth/caterpillar damage to chrysanthemum leaves (from a Kodachrome by The Ohio State University Extension Service).

Moth/caterpillar.—There are several pests that are moths as adults and caterpillars as youngsters. Often both forms of pest are not seen because their working hours are at night. They spend their days in shady, moist locations. Larva feeding damage is to the stems, leaves, or flowers, depending on the type of moth/caterpillar. Sometimes the damage caused is similar to the damage caused by slugs.

Slug.—The slug is very common on crops like garden plants that are grown on the ground. The type of feeding damage is similar to the damage caused by caterpillars. However, slugs leave a telltale slime trail from daytime lair to nighttime feast. The slug is not an insect.

Leafminer.—Adult leafminers are tiny, gray flies that are not observed easily. The larva, that develops from an egg laid in leaf tissues, feeds between the upper and lower surfaces, causing the characteristic tunnel as feeding progresses.

Mealybug.—The mealybug appears to be small clusters of white cotton tucked into stem and leaf depressions. It is wingless and seems to be motionless. It is a common pest of foliage plants.

Scale.—There are various kinds of scale. Generally, they are tan to brown, round, slightly raised spots about ¼ inch in diameter that seem to be stuck on stem or leaf surfaces. They are wingless and seem to be motionless. Scale are common pests of foliage plants.

Fungus gnat.—Adult fungus gnats are tiny, gray flies that are noticeable because they band together in flocks that appear to be floating fog or puffs of smoke. The main damage to plants is caused by larvae feeding on the roots.

Garden symphylan.—Symphylans are not insects. They are tiny, many-legged pests that live in the soil and feed on roots. If they are present, when the soil is disturbed they scurry rapidly for cover in the soil.

The damage to roots may be similar to the effects of the feeding of fungus gnat larvae, but the scurrying is telltale of symphylans. There is a rather harmless insect that is white and symphylan-size, but it moves by springing. Its common name is springtail.

Fig. 5-25. Leafminer damage to a chrysanthemum leaf (Yoder Bros., Inc., photograph).

Fig. 5-26. Mealybugs on a grape ivy stem.

Fig. 5-27. Scales on schefflera.

Pathogens and Disease

The main means for pathogen and disease control are to eliminate pathogens and to provide conditions that are not suitable for the growth of pathogens.

Eliminating pathogens.—Pathogens can be eliminated from soils by steaming and from plant-propagating stock by culture-indexing. It generally is not possible to eliminate all air-borne pathogens. Also, some pathogens may appear by way of diseased plants brought into greenhouses or by way of infected pests. The growth of air-borne pathogens may be controlled by (1) using nonsusceptible cultivars and (2) providing surroundings that are not suitable for pathogen growth. It usually is not possible to grow cultivars that are not susceptible to all pathogen growth, but it is possible through proper control of the plants' surroundings, to prevent the start of many diseases. Critical surroundings to be controlled are sunlight, moisture, heat, and ventilation.

The basic program of the use of pathogen-free crop starters, steamed soil, and proper control of surroundings results in generally disease-free crops. Pathogen control by fungicide or bactericide should be needed only when there is some fault in the basic program. If there is evidence of disease, proper control is possible only if the cause of disease is positively identified.

Use of Pesticides

The use of pesticides is controlled by federal, state, and province regulations. The following general comments should not be in conflict with any of the governmental regulations.

The use of pesticides is for limiting or stopping the activities of pests or pathogens and thus allowing the successful production of crops. The *active ingredient* of the pesticide is the effective material for control of the pest or pathogen. The purposes of the other material in pesticides are for (1) diluting the active ingredient, (2) keeping the active ingredient in suspension or solution, and (3) dispersing or propelling the active ingredient. Although pesticides are used for good reasons, some damage can result from improper usage. The damage may be caused by either the active ingredient or the other materials in the pesticide, or both.

Fig. 5-28. Botrytis blight of a geranium leaf.

Fig. 5-29. Botrytis blight of older chrysanthemum florets.

Fig. 5-30. Botrytis blight of older geranium florets.

Fig. 5-31. Powdery mildew on rose leaves.

Fig. 5-32. Stages of development of downy mildew of rose leaves.

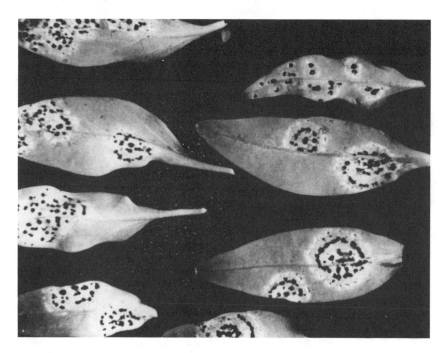

Fig. 5-33. Rust disease of snapdragon leaves (from a Kodachrome by C. W. Ellet).

Fig. 5-34. Stem and root rot of chrysanthemum. Rotted plants are at bottom center and left. A healthy plant is at bottom right.

Fig. 5-35. Stem and root rot of chrysanthemum plants at center and at right. A healthy plant is at left.

Fig. 5-36. Root rot of Easter lily
at right.

Damage to plants from the active ingredient in a pesticide can be caused by the application of too much pesticide, either because an excess amount of the pesticide was placed in the applicator or because the plants were treated an excess period of time. Damage to people may result from either lack of protection from the pesticide or improper handling or applying of the pesticide.

There are possibilities of plant damage from the use of pesticides that contain oils or propellants. The damage from oils occurs when the oils enter the plant surfaces and kill tissues. The damage from propellants occurs when growers apply aerosol pesticides too closely to plants.

Weed Control

Weeds can be eliminated in greenhouse soils by steaming. When crop periods are less than one year and when soil steaming is used between crops, there should not be weed problems in bed or bench soils. Weeds may be a problem in the bed and bench soils of crops with long cropping periods.

Hand-pulling or hoeing is the weed-elimination method used for walks, for soils of long-term crops, and for the areas immediately outside greenhouses. The pulling or hoeing has to be done at the early stages of weed growth.

Herbicides (weed killers) are not safe for use in or around greenhouses.

Chapter 6

CUT-FLOWER CROPS

With the exception of rose flower production, cut-flower production in the United States and Canada is concentrated mainly in the southwestern and southern United States. Rose flowers are produced and marketed in local areas throughout the United States and Canada.

The basics of culture for several cut-flower crops are given here. Trade periodicals and literature from trade organizations, Cooperative Extension Service, and plant vendors may be used for current recommendations.

BULBS

Daffodil (narcissus) and iris may be used for cut-flower production from midwinter to the spring.

Daffodil

The main cultivars used for daffodil production are trumpet types, but large and small cupped cultivars may be used to some extent. The cropping period is from late December to mid-January for precooled bulbs and from late January through February for regular bulbs.

The bulbs, which are produced mainly in the northwestern United States, are graded by type and size. The type is either single nose or

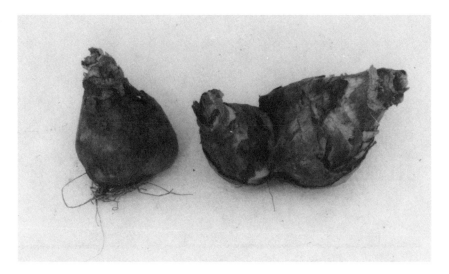

Fig. 6-1. Daffodil bulbs for starting crops. A single-nose, #1-grade bulb is shown at left. A double-nose, #1-grade bulb is shown at right.

double nose. A single-nose bulb consists of a solitary bulb that produces only one flower. A double-nose bulb consists of the mother bulb with one or more daughter bulbs attached. Flowers may be produced by the daughter as well as by the mother.

The double-nose, #1-grade bulbs are usually used in greenhouse production. Regular bulbs are shipped in late September, and precooled bulbs are shipped in October. The bulbs should be planted as soon as they arrive.

The bulbs are planted bulb-to-bulb in boxes, with the noses just above the soil. After the bulbs are thoroughly watered, the boxes are placed in refrigerated storage at 50°F for about two weeks (until there is good root development) and then at 35°F for the balance of the storage period. Precooled bulbs may be removed from storage for forcing starting in early December and continuing until early January. For satisfactory forcing, the flower bud must be developed enough so it is out of the bulb nose. The amount of flower bud development is determined by carefully squeezing the leaves just above the bulb nose. Greenhouse forcing time shortens from four weeks to three weeks as the season progresses.

From about mid-January on, regular bulbs may be removed from storage for the start of forcing. Boxes of bulbs are brought into the greenhouse at regular intervals to provide a succession of flowering.

Daffodils need regular irrigation, but no fertilizer is used during the forcing period.

Daffodil flowers are harvested by cutting through the leaf bases and the flower stem just above the bulb nose. The flowers may be harvested when fully mature or in tight bud, depending on how they will be used. Tight-bud harvesting is used if shipping is involved. After harvesting, the flowers are bunched, vased in water, and refrigerated at about 45°F.

Iris

There are several types of iris. The cultivars used for greenhouse flower production are commonly called Dutch iris. Flower production may be from early December to April for the bulbs planted in early October to February. The bulbs are mainly produced in the northwestern United States. They are graded by size in terms of centimeters of circumference. The size bulbs commonly used in greenhouse flower production

Fig. 6-2. At left, an iris flower bud showing color. At right, a mature flower.

are 9-10 and 10-11. The bulb producers usually handle the various bulb storage procedures and ship the properly processed bulbs to growers at the correct times for planting. When bulbs are forced at 60°F, the crop time is about 10 weeks.

Iris should be planted in beds or benches. A continuous supply of water is needed for iris, and this can be provided better when the bulbs are in beds or benches than it can be when they are in boxes. Lack of water can cause damaged flower buds. The standard planting distance is about 2 inches by 4 inches, but variations are used. Iris bulbs have convex bottoms and pointed tops. Planting is done by gently pushing the bulbs into the soil, with the tips left just above the soil. Fertilizer is not used in iris flower production.

The flowers are harvested when color appears in the tight buds. The flowers are bunched and then placed in water in refrigerators.

CARNATION

Widespread carnation production in the United States and Canada was greatly affected by improved long-distance shipping. Most of the

Fig. 6-3. A standard carnation flower is at left, and a spray carnation flower is at right.

production is located in favorable climate areas like California, South America, Mexico, and Central America.

Types and Areas of Production

Carnation types are the large, solitary standards and the small, spray miniatures. The major part of production is in standard-type carnation. The main production area is California.

Cropping Period

The cropping period may be one or two years. Planting is usually from spring to summer, and main flowering is from late fall through spring. Standard carnation are usually grown as two-year crops, with one-half of the growing area replanted yearly. Miniature carnation are often one-year crops.

Crop-Starter Plants, Planting, and Pinching

The crop-starter plants are stem-tip rooted cuttings that are purchased from propagation specialists. The cuttings originate from culture-indexed stock plants so growers are able to start their crops with pathogen-free plants.

Each of the rooted cuttings is given about 50 square inches of area. A typical spacing is 6 inches between the plants and 8 inches between the rows. The cuttings are planted as shallowly as possible so they will be less susceptible to stem diseases. If some cuttings topple because of the shallow planting, they are easily reset. The soil is thoroughly watered after planting, and then to further avoid disease, misting, irrigation, and heating are carefully regulated so the soil surface dries readily.

The plants are pinched within a few weeks after planting. The plants must have grown enough so the internode above the sixth pair of leaves is clear for making the pinch as carnation tip leaves extend upward beyond the stem tip. If pinching is attempted too soon, only the leaves instead of the stem tip may be pinched. Because the rate of growth in a planting is a variable, all of the plants cannot be pinched at the same time. Removal of the stem tip by pinching causes branching, giving a potential of future flower production of one flower per branch. Usually some of the shoots from the first pinch are also pinched to further increase branching and flower production during the winter.

Temperature and Photoperiod

Generally, night temperature is maintained at 50°F and day temperatures at 55° to 60°F.

Carnation flowers mature more rapidly during long photoperiods than they do during short photoperiods. Some growers use incandescent lamps from dusk to dawn for two to three weeks during the winter to advance the flowering of some stems from summer to the generally better market in late spring.

Problems

Carnation are susceptible to several serious diseases. It is very important to start with pathogen-free cuttings, to use thoroughly steamed soil, and to avoid introducing pathogens.

The common carnation pests are twospotted mite, aphid, and thrips. Growers have to recognize pest problems in the early stages and make proper treatment promptly.

A growth situation called splitting reduces the sales value of the flowers. Flower splitting is solely a carnation problem that occurs when conditions cause development of an excessive number of petals and splitting of the calyx. Cultivars vary considerably in their tendency to split. Splitting may be avoided by growing cultivars that seldom split, by controlling temperature carefully, or by banding each calyx before flower maturity.

Disbudding and Harvesting

As the terminal flower develops, lateral flower buds also form. With standard carnation cultivars, it is desirable to have a solitary large flower per stem, so the lateral flower buds are disbudded. The disbudding must be done as soon as the buds can be removed conveniently without damage to flower, leaves, or stem.

Fig. 6-4. Several networks need
to be used to support carnation stems
upright.

With miniature cultivars, it is desirable to have several flowers per
stem. This will occur when flower buds are not removed, but with many
cultivars, flowering is more uniform if the terminal flower bud is disbudded at an early stage of development. The terminal flower buds of
miniature cultivars are commonly disbudded.

Flowers are usually harvested when the petals are fully expanded
to hemisphere shape, but in some instances flowers are harvested when
color shows in the buds. The bud-harvest method provides some
economies in harvesting and grading time as well as in shipping costs.

The customer, however, does have additional costs in time and space before the flowers are ready to use after they are received.

The place of cutting the stem usually is varied with the season of the year. At harvest time, there may be two or three shoots developing lower on the stem. If the stem is cut above these shoots, the flower stem will be shorter, but future flower production will be greater and mature sooner. This type of cut is often made in the fall and in the early winter. In winter and spring harvesting, the cuts are usually made in order to give longer flower stems.

Carnation harvesting may be only two or three times per week.

CHRYSANTHEMUM

Chrysanthemum production is a classic example of the dramatic effect new information can have on an industry. Until the relationship of photoperiod and flowering was understood in 1930, chrysanthemum was only a fall crop. After several years of trials and development, chrysanthemum is a main year-round crop.

Types and Areas of Production

Chrysanthemum cut-flower production may be with large-flowered standard, or commercial, cultivars or with small-flowered spray cultivars. Both of these types of chrysanthemum are generally available in more than one color. Flower colors are classed in four broad groups— white, yellow, bronze, and pink. The bronze group includes oranges and reds, and the pink group includes lavenders and purples.

The flowers in each size type have various forms. Some common forms of the large-size chrysanthemum are: (1) *incurved*—ball shaped; (2) *reflexed*—flat topped; (3) *spider*—reflexed, tubular florets; and (4) *Fuji*—upright, tubular florets.

Some common forms of the small-flowered chrysanthemum are: (1) *pompon*—ball shaped; (2) *single*—daisy-like; (3) *anemone*— daisy-like with cushion centers; and (4) *decorative*—flat topped.

Chrysanthemum plants also vary in the length of time needed for flower development. They are classified by the number of weeks needed for flowering after the start of short photoperiods. These classifications are known as response groups. Most of the cultivars used in cut-flower production are classified in either 9- or 10-week response groups. Vendors of mum cuttings publish schedules for year-round flower-crop production. For the weekly flowering dates, the schedules list recommended cultivars and dates for (1) planting, (2) long photoperiods, and (3) short photoperiods.

The main greenhouse production of chrysanthemum cut flowers is in California. Also, in Florida there is considerable production of spray chrysanthemum under plastic screen from fall to spring.

Cropping Period

Chrysanthemum cut-flower crops may be grown single-stem (not pinched) or branched (pinched). The crop period is about two weeks longer if the plants are pinched. References here are to single-stem crops. Depending on which cultivars are used, the crop period may be as short as 10 weeks in the summer or as long as 14 weeks in the winter.

When the crop is harvested, the plants are removed and discarded, and new mum crops are planted. Usually the mum cut-flower areas are continuously in cut-mum production year-round.

Crop-Starter Plants and Planting

Generally, the crop-starter plants are stem-tip rooted cuttings. In some favorable climates, stem-tip unrooted cuttings are used. The cuttings are usually purchased from propagation specialists who take cuttings from culture-indexed plants so the crops can be started with pathogen-free plants. Common planting distances are 4 inches by 6 inches for single-stem crops and 6 inches by 8 inches for pinched crops.

The cuttings are planted as shallowly as possible to avoid stem diseases. Cuttings for pinched crops are pinched above four to six leaves about two weeks after planting. About two weeks after pinching, the two best shoots are retained, and the other shoots are pruned.

Temperature and Photoperiod

Chrysanthemum are often grown at a 60°F night temperature and at 65° to 70°F day temperatures.

Fig. 6-5. Chrysanthemum cut-flower rotation. The most recent planting is shown at bottom, progressing to a crop ready to harvest at top.

After planting, it is necessary to have stem and leaf growth for one to several weeks so the stems will be suitably long for cut flowers. If the natural daylengths are not long enough after planting, electric lighting must be used for long photoperiods. When the leafy growth is about 12 inches high, short photoperiods need to be provided so the flowers can develop. If the natural days are not short enough, light has to be excluded from the plants for part of each day until the flowers develop.

Problems

Stem and root diseases can usually be avoided by the use of

pathogen-free cuttings, steamed soil, shallow planting, and proper irrigation. Floret blight of some large-flowered cultivars can be avoided if ventilation and heating are handled properly.

Pests usually cannot be completely avoided. Growers have to inspect the plants continuously for the first indications of pests and use the necessary pesticides at once. Common pests are twospotted mite, aphid, leafminer, and thrips.

Temperature and photoperiod problems are rather common. For example, during hot weather, flowering may be delayed and plants continue to grow in length. Some large-flowered cultivars are easily sunburned in hot weather unless they are shaded from the sunlight.

Variable photoperiods caused by imperfect exclusion of light or by failure of lighting systems can cause flower deformities.

Disbudding and Harvesting

The lateral flower buds of large-flowered mums are disbudded as soon as they are large enough to be handled. The lateral flower buds

Fig. 6-6. A single network is used to support chrysanthemum stems.

**Fig. 6-7. Standard (commercial)
mum flowers to be harvested.**

of spray mums are not disbudded, but many growers do disbud the terminal flower bud as soon as it can be handled.

The flowers are harvested when the florets are mature. The stems are cut just above the ground. There is some variability in the time of flowering, but usually an entire planting can be cut in one week. The mature flowers are harvested daily.

ROSE

Rose plant growth and flowering are faster than that of chrysanthemum and much faster than carnation plant growth and flower development. Rose cut flowers also have a short period of life after harvest. For this reason, it is important that rose cut flowers are available to customers as soon as possible after harvest. Closeness to market is very important in rose flower production.

Types and Areas of Production

The types of rose produced are hybrid tea and floribunda (sweetheart), with more than 90 percent of the production from tea plants. Tea-rose plants have large solitary flowers with long stems. If lateral flower buds develop, they are disbudded. The tea rose that produces somewhat smaller flowers may be called an intermediate.

Floribunda have smaller flowers and shorter stems than the tea rose and frequently develop lateral flower buds, which may or may not be disbudded. If the lateral flower buds are not disbudded, there will be a spray of flowers per stem.

The quantity of flowers produced per plant per year varies with the type of rose, the individual cultivars, and the growing conditions and procedures. Yearly flower production per plant may be about 20 flowers for large-flowered tea, 30 for intermediate, and 40 or more for floribunda.

Roses, Inc., is the international association for commercial rose flower producers. Its 1987–88 members who market flowers in the United States and Canada report that about 90 percent of the producing plants are in the United States; 8 percent in Canada; and 2 percent in Colombia, Mexico, and Peru. Of the rose flower–producing plants in the United States, about 50 percent are in California greenhouses. About 32 percent of the flower-producing plants are in greenhouses in Colorado, Indiana, New York, Ohio, Oregon, and Pennsylvania. The remaining 18 percent of the flower-producing plants are in greenhouses in Connecticut, Hawaii, Kentucky, Massachusetts, Michigan, Minnesota, New Hampshire, New Jersey, Utah, Virginia, Wisconsin, Alabama, Arizona, Arkansas, Florida, Georgia, Idaho, Illinois, Iowa, Maryland, Missouri, Montana, New Mexico, North Carolina, Rhode Island, and Washington.

Of the rose flower–producing plants in Canada, the approximate distribution of plants by province is Ontario, 69 percent; Nova Scotia, 11 percent; British Columbia, 7 percent; Quebec, 6 percent; Alberta, 5 percent; and New Brunswick, 2 percent.

Cropping Period

Rose plants are usually cropped for about five years and then discarded and replaced with new plants. During the cropping period, the main work with the plants involves pinching, harvesting, and pruning. The work with the plants is scheduled so the needed quantity of flowers can be harvested uniformly year-round, with additional amounts harvested for special marketing periods like Sweetest Day, Christmas, Valentine's Day, Easter, Secretary's Day, and Mother's Day. Plantings in February may produce some flowers for Mother's Day—thus replacing the flowers that would have been harvested from the removed plants. Later plantings in the spring are scheduled to replace the flowers that would have been produced from May to July by the removed plants and by the other plants that are pruned from May through July.

Rose plants are pruned yearly so plant height is maintained within working distance. The shoots that develop from the pruned plants are pinched, and the flower production from these plants resumes in the fall.

Flowers can develop in six to eight weeks from shoots that form in the stems that remain after harvesting or pinching. However, many of the shoots that develop after harvest are pinched rather than allowed to flower immediately. Pinching may be used to schedule flowering for a later date, to cause development of more stems and leaves per plant, or to develop longer flower stems.

Crop-Starter Plants, Planting, and Pinching

Rose crops are started with dormant, started-eye plants. Generally, the large, triple-X grade of plants is used for greenhouse flower production. These are bud-grafted plants that are field-grown mainly in California. The plants are refrigerated after digging and must be kept cold until planting time. The plants can be shipped from late December on.

Common planting times are in mid-February, after the Valentine's Day crop has been harvested from the plants that will be removed, and in mid-May, after the Mother's Day crop has been harvested. Upon their arrival, the plants are inspected for frost damage and for the stage of development of the stem buds. The buds should be starting to swell at planting time. If the stem buds are small, the plants may be kept warm and moist for a few days before planting .

The roots are pruned to about 3 inches before planting. Various spacing methods are used, but each rose plant is generally allowed

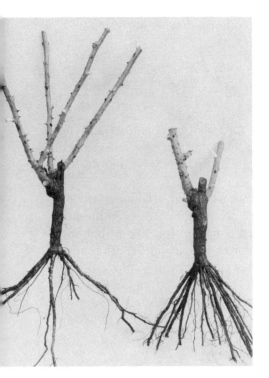

Fig. 6-8. Rose dormant, started-eye plants to be planted.

about 1 square foot of bed or bench area. A trowel is usually used in planting. A suitable-size hole is dug, the plant is lowered into the hole, the roots are spread, and soil is backfilled around the roots. After the initial watering, the soil is allowed to dry somewhat before irrigating again. The aboveground canes, however, need to be kept moist so that the swelling of stem buds and the emergence of shoots proceed promptly.

The shoots that develop after planting are pinched to develop well-branched plants. Often each plant will have one to three thick shoots and several thin shoots. The thin shoots require the most care. If the thin shoots are pinched early, thicker shoots and larger leaves will develop. The shoots that form after these pinches may also need to be pinched to make further improvement in shoot growth.

The thick shoots may be allowed to grow to flower bud and then given a soft pinch. In some instances, a flower may be harvested from the best shoots instead of pinching.

Temperature, Lighting, and Carbon Dioxide

Generally, the night temperature for rose plants is 60°F and the day temperature from 65° to 70°F, but temperatures may be increased to hasten flower maturity or decreased to delay flower maturity, as needed for the market.

During the winter in northern locations, flower production can be increased by high-intensity supplementary lighting. The lighting may be from dusk to dawn from fall to spring. Some growers use the lighting 24 hours per day when sunlight is scarce. Increasing the amount of carbon dioxide in the air at this time of the year can improve flower quality as well as increase production. Even though the lighting and carbon dioxide may be beneficial, they are added expense, so rose growers have to compare the cost to the proposed revenue to decide if the procedure is economical.

Problems

Powdery mildew is a common disease of rose plants, but it can generally be avoided when heating and ventilating are regulated so the plants are warmer than the air. When sunlight is available, the plants usually are warmer than the air. At night and on cloudy days, heating systems have to be activated soon enough so that the relationship of plant-air temperature is maintained. Providing continuous air movement also helps to avoid powdery mildew. When powdery mildew does occur, it may be controlled with some fungicides.

Twospotted mite is a persistent rose pest. Plants should be continuously inspected for evidence of the mites, and proper pesticides used promptly.

Some rose stems do not terminate with flowers. These stems are commonly called *blind shoots.* Instead of developing flower buds, these stems get progressively thinner and seem to terminate as pointed stems. Blind shoots occur mainly when sunlight is scarce, but the amount of blind shoots varies with the cultivars and the cultural conditions. There

Fig. 6-9. Rose greenhouse in continuous production of flowers.

may not be as many blind shoots when irrigations are spaced far enough apart so there is continuous root growth. Cleaning greenhouse coverings and adding high-intensity lighting may reduce the amount of blind shoots.

Harvesting

Generally, rose flowers are harvested when the petals start to unfurl, but there are differences in cultivars. Rose growers give specific instructions to harvesters about the correct stage of flower development for harvesting each cultivar at their greenhouses. The time of rose harvest may vary with the season of the year, but it is always twice a day, generally the first thing in the morning and during the late afternoon. In hot weather, an additional harvest may be made at about noon. Some growers find that daylight savings time doesn't fit well with rose harvesting because there is an hour longer for the flowers to mature overnight.

There must be a good understanding about the position of cut on the stem. There are two considerations in deciding where to cut—the effect on flower stem length and the effect on plant growth and future flower production. The length-of-stem consideration is constant—the longer the stem, the higher the selling price. The welfare-of-the-plant considerations vary mainly with seasonal growing conditions, the need for additional flower production, when the plant will be pruned, and when the plants will be discarded. With all of this in mind, the rose grower makes the decisions from week to week about the position for cutting the flowers. The cutting instructions that are passed along to the harvesters may be something like "cut above two fives," "cut above one five," or "cut below the hook." The term "five" refers to a five-leaflet leaf. Greenhouse rose plants have three-leaflet and five-leaflet leaves, and there is a typical progression of these leaves. If a flowering stem is viewed from the point where it developed from the plant, it can be seen that usually one incomplete leaf is followed by one three-leaflet leaf and then by several five-leaflet leaves. Toward the stem tip, there are one or two three-leaflet leaves, one incomplete leaf, and then the flower. The directions "cut above two fives" and "leave two fives" both refer to making the cut just above the second five-leaflet leaf from the base of the stem. Cutting above two fives increases the height of the plant and the number of leaves on the plant. This type of cutting is common from late summer to midwinter. From late winter to summer, the common instructions may be either "cut to one five" or "cut below the hook." "Cutting below the hook" is making the cut above the five-leaflet leaf that is below the place of origin of the flowering stem from the plant. Rose growers may give various other harvesting instructions. The important point is that their harvesting instructions have to be followed very carefully.

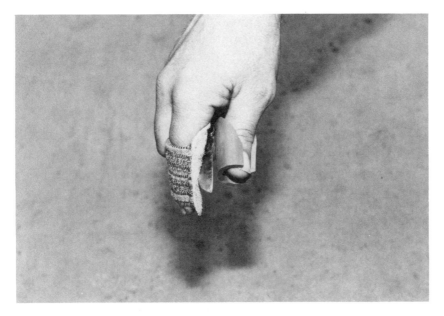

Fig. 6-10. Finger and thumb stalls and proper grip on knife for harvesting flowers.

Fig. 6-11. Cutting a rose flower stem above a five-leaflet leaf.

After harvest, the rose flowers are placed in vase water that is treated for prompt entry of water into the stems. Currently, vase water is adjusted to pH 3.5 with citric acid, but continuing research may develop even better water treatments.

SNAPDRAGON

It is difficult to ship snapdragon because of two of its characteristics. It is succulent and easily crushed, and its stem tips turn upward *(geotropism)* when snapdragon is shipped in a horizontal position. These characteristics are probably the reasons snapdragon has not become a distant-production crop. Snapdragon was a companion local crop of carnation and chrysanthemum, but it has not survived well alone in local production after carnation and chrysanthemum have become distant-production crops.

Types and Areas of Production

Hybridizers have developed cultivars for snapdragon flowering in different seasons of the year. These cultivars are classified into four groups for flowering: (1) winter, (2) late fall to early winter, (3) spring or fall, and (4) summer. The groups 3 and 4 cultivars are more adaptable for greenhouse rotations because of shorter crop times and seasons of flowering.

Cropping Period

The length of time from planting to harvesting is as long as 23 weeks for winter flowering and as short as 8 weeks for summer flowering. Seed has to be sown about one month before the planting date.

If carbon-dioxide additions are used to about 1,200 ppm for winter crops, production time is decreased by three to four weeks.

These cropping times are for unpinched crops. If plants are pinched, only half the number of plants are needed, and the cropping time is increased by about two weeks.

Fig. 6-12. Snapdragon seedlings to be planted in flower production benches.

Crop-Starter Plants, Planting, and Pinching

Snapdragon crops are started with seedlings. Whenever possible, the seedlings should be grown by the snapdragon grower so the seedlings can be transplanted directly from seed flat to crop bench without any shipping involved. The seedlings are transplanted about one month after sowing, and they are tiny—about 1 inch high.

For spring-to-fall crops, the seedlings are planted at about 4- to 5-inch spacing. Because of the small size of the plants, the soil must be cultivated sufficiently so the soil particles are uniformly small.

If a pinched crop is grown, the plants are spaced about 6 by 8 inches, and the pinch is made above four pairs of leaves about two weeks after planting.

Temperature

The spring-to-fall crops are grown at a 60°F night temperature and

Fig. 6-13. Snapdragon flower at the harvesting stage.

65° to 70°F day temperatures. The groups 1 and 2 cultivars grown from fall to spring, are usually grown at a 50°F night temperature and at 55°F to 60°F day temperatures.

Problems

Snapdragon stem and root diseases can usually be avoided if the soil is thoroughly steamed, the soil drains readily, and the soil is allowed to dry somewhat between irrigations.

Gray mold infection of stem, leaves, and flowers may occur in humid surroundings. This problem can usually be avoided when the plants are kept warmer than the air by proper heating and ventilating.

Aphids are a common pest, but they can be controlled when pesticides are promptly applied.

Harvesting

The lower florets of the flower cluster mature first, and floret maturing progresses gradually upward. The flowers are harvested when about six florets per cluster are mature. The stems are cut just above the ground. The entire planting is harvested in about one week. The plants are discarded after the harvest.

Chapter 7

POT-PLANT CROPS

There are constant changes in crops and procedures. Crop-starter vendors, trade periodicals, and Cooperative Extension Service bulletins may be used for current information.

AZALEA

Azalea may be grown as a year-round crop in greenhouses, but year-round production is generally more economical in the southern and coastal areas of the United States, where part of the production can be outdoors or with minimum protection from the weather.

Growers who include azalea among their crops may use any of the following cropping methods: (1) The natural-season method uses liner crop starters in the spring for production of mature plants by fall. Sales are from December through April. (2) The budded-plant method uses mature plants that are received in the fall from specialists. These plants may need cool-temperature treatment before forcing. Sales may be December through April. (3) The year-round method uses mature plants that may be received at any time from specialists. These plants are ready for forcing.

Natural-season production is discussed here.

Cropping Period

Azalea started in May have developed mature flower buds by October. The plants are refrigerated and removed for forcing from November on. The latest forcing may be in April for early May flowering.

Crop-Starter Plants and Planting

Various size crop-starter plants are used, depending on the desired size of the mature flowering plants. The smaller plants may be bare-root liners, and the larger starter plants may be knocked out of pots. On arrival, the plants should be placed in a cool, shaded location until time for potting.

Soil used for potting is coarse, fibrous peat moss. Firm potting is needed. The potted plants are set pot-to-pot and are well-watered.

May–July

Temperature.—Temperatures should be 70°F during nights and 75° to 80°F during days.

Shearing and spacing.—Shearing (pinching) is done in late June. Usually, about 1 inch of stem tips is removed with knife or shears.

Spacing for 6½-inch pots may be on 12-inch centers.

A growth material to promote branching may be applied within two days of shearing.

August–September

Temperature.—Temperatures should be 65°F during nights and 70° to 75°F during days.

Growth regulator.—Growth regulator should be applied during the first week and then again one week later.

Late September–Early October

The plants are moved to refrigerators where the temperatures are kept at 36° to 45°F. The plants are set plant-to-plant.

Fig. 7-1. Mature azalea to be marketed.

Forcing

Temperature.—Temperatures should be 60°F during nights and 65° to 70°F during days.

Starting.—Christmas plants—start November 1 (use giberellic acid spray); Valentine's Day plants—start December 26; Easter plants—start four weeks before; Mother's Day plants—start three weeks before.

CHRYSANTHEMUM

Types and Areas of Production

Chrysanthemum cultivars vary in the length of time needed for flowering after the start of short photoperiods. For year-round production, cultivars that flower 9 and 10 weeks after the start of short photoperiods generally are suitable. These year-round pot mums are grown mainly for indoor use. However, it is possible that some of these cultivars may be used as garden and landscape plants in warm climates. In colder climates, 7- and 8-week cultivars may be grown for outdoor use; they are known as garden mums.

Various flower types and colors of chrysanthemum are used for pot plants.

Chrysanthemum cultivars also vary in height and are classed as short, medium, and tall growers. Production procedures vary accordingly so cultivars of each class mature at about the same height.

Pot mums are widely grown throughout the United States and Canada. There are areas of concentrated production in the southwestern United States.

Cropping Period

The length of the cropping period varies with the season of the year, the climate, the cultivar, and the production method. The cropping period may vary from 8 to 13 weeks.

Pot-mum growers usually start crops regularly so they will have a uniform quantity of plants available for marketing during each week year-round. Additional quantities are scheduled for marketing for holidays and special events.

Crop-Starter Plants, Planting, and Pinching

Rooted cuttings are usually used for starting crops, but unrooted cuttings are used by some growers in favorable climates and during favorable seasons of the year. The cuttings are usually purchased from specialist propagators who can supply pathogen-free cuttings. Some growers use the cuttings to start stock plants so they can produce their own cuttings. These growers plan to replace their stock plants often enough to avoid disease problems.

For year-round pot mums, 6½-inch pots are usually used. From three to five cuttings are used per pot, depending on the season of the year, the cultivars, the production methods, and the market demands. The cuttings are set equidistantly around the edge of the pot, and the cuttings are planted as shallowly as possible.

Fig. 7-2. A case of chrysanthemum rooted cuttings to be potted. A sample cutting is displayed at top.

Garden mums are usually grown in 6-inch pots, with one cutting planted in the center of the pot. They should be pinched twice.

Regular pot mums are pinched to produce shorter and bushier plants. To regulate the height of the mature plant, the time of pinch is scheduled by the number of long and short photoperiods between planting and pinching. For example, short-growing cultivars may be supplied three weeks of long photoperiods between planting and pinching; medium-growing cultivars two weeks; and tall-growing cultivars one week of long photoperiods and one week of short photoperiods before pinching. Soft pinches are used that remove only the top ½ inch of the stems.

Temperature and Photoperiod

For one to three weeks after planting (depending on the cultivar and the season), the plants should be in long photoperiods and in 65°F night temperature with bottom heating. Then, the plants may be in 60°F night temperature and short photoperiods until flowering. The long photoperiods cause the amount of stem growth needed for the mature plants.

Fig. 7-3. Chrysanthemum set pot-to-pot after potting. This area provides bottom heating and long photoperiods.

Fig. 7-4. Chrysanthemum from pot-to-pot area set in final spacing in production greenhouse.

Problems

Chrysanthemum are subject to several diseases, but these can usually be avoided by the use of pathogen-free cuttings, steamed soil, and shallow planting.

Some common pests are twospotted mite, aphid, leafminer, and various caterpillar/moth pests.

Flowering can be affected by wrong or variable photoperiods and by either too-low or too-high temperatures.

Disbudding and Harvesting

Two types of disbudding may be used. If the objective is to have solitary large flowers per stem, all of the lateral flower buds are removed as soon as they can be handled. If the objective is to have a spray of flowers per stem, only the terminal flower bud is removed as soon as it can be handled.

Usually the mum pot plants mature uniformly, and the entire crop can be marketed at one time. The flowers should be well developed at the time of marketing.

Fig. 7-5. Chrysanthemum pot-plant greenhouse a few weeks before harvest.

FOLIAGE PLANTS

General production is in Florida and in some other locations in the southern and southwestern United States where part of the production is outdoors or with limited protection from climate. Pot-plant growers in colder climates do much of their foliage-plant business on a buy-and-sell basis. Depending on the extent of their business, they may purchase by telephone, through brokers, or by personal buying trips to the foliage-plant production areas.

Some pot-plant growers have established foliage-plant production areas in the South to supply the foliage-plant needs of their northern greenhouses.

Some northern greenhouse operators deal only with foliage-plant crops, but many greenhouse producers of flowering pot plants also have foliage plants for sale. The foliage-plant business varies with the size of the plants. General size classifications are (1) *small*—seedlings, rooted cuttings, and plants in 3-inch or smaller pots; (2) *medium*—plants in 6- to 10-inch pots; (3) *large*—plants with 14- to 48-inch pots or root balls.

Fig. 7-6. Small foliage plants for gardens.

Fig. 7-7. Foliage-plant dish gardens.

Small plants.—Greenhouse pot-plant growers use small foliage plants for making dish gardens of assorted plants or for selling single plants in 3- or 4-inch pots. The dish gardens are sold mainly to flower-shop operators. Flower-shop operators also buy plants in 3-inch pots for making their own dish gardens.

Garden and general-merchandise store operators usually buy foliage plants in 3- and 4-inch pots for sale to consumers.

Medium plants.—Usually medium and large plants are neither repotted nor grown to a larger size. They are considered marketable shortly after they are received. The medium plants may be sold to various types of retailers—flower shop, garden store, general-merchandise, and interiorscape.

Large plants.—The larger plants are mainly sold to interiorscapers and to some operators of flower shops.

GARDEN PLANTS

Garden plants produced in greenhouses are mainly propagated by seed and grown and sold in packs. Geranium is propagated by both seed and cuttings. The cutting-grown geranium are grown and sold in 4-inch pots.

Greenhouse pot-plant growers may be involved in garden-plant production as specialist propagators (plug producers), plug and pack producers, pack producers, or garden-plant pot and hanging-basket producers. The pot-plant growers' involvement in garden-plant production depends on how it fits in with other types of pot-plant production. Garden-plant growing is a spring business, but the arrival of spring varies with location in the country. In warm climates, spring may arrive before Easter and Mother's Day. In cold climates, there may be competition for greenhouse production space for Easter, Mother's Day, and garden-plant crops.

Plug producers.—Because plug trays can be satisfactorily packed and shipped, plug producers may be able to ship to spring pack producers in various areas of the country. It is possible that because of the several spring areas that they serve, plug producers' equipment and space may be in plug production for six months or longer.

The approximate lengths of time from sowing to mature plugs for some of the garden plants are 4 weeks for impatiens and tomato; 6 weeks for fibrous begonia, marigold, and petunia; and 12 weeks for geranium.

Plug and pack producers.—These garden-plant growers plan to produce the plugs for the packs that they will market. Generally, they produce quantities of packs and deliver them within a radius of several hundred miles by the truck load.

Their customers are retail operators of garden stores, general-merchandise stores, and outdoor landscape services.

Pack producers.—Plugs purchased from specialists are crop starters for the pack producers. The length of time from planting to marketing may be from two to six weeks, depending on the cultivar, the desired size of the plants, and the weather conditions.

The pack producers' customers may be local retail operators of flower shops and of independent general-merchandise stores.

Pot and hanging-basket producers.—Plants from packs are the usual crop starters used by pot and hanging-basket producers. The

Fig. 7-8. Plug-tray propagating room.

Fig. 7-9. Shipping method for plug trays.

length of time from planting to marketing may be about 2 to 4 weeks for 4-inch pots and about 10 weeks for hanging baskets.

These producers' customers may be local retail operators of flower shops, garden stores, general-merchandise stores, and outdoor landscape services.

EASTER LILY

The lily bulbs for starting the crops may be shipped either from the West Coast fields after digging or from refrigerated storage six weeks after digging. Because of variable dates for Easter, the start of forcing has to be adjusted accordingly.

The main preforcing procedure is the placement of the bulbs in temperatures below 50°F for at least six weeks to allow the crop to flower in time for Easter. This cool treatment may be provided before or after potting. During this storage period, the bulbs must be in moist surroundings.

Lily bulbs are deeply potted.

October potting.—When the bulbs are potted directly after harvest from the fields, they are watered and placed in about 60°F night temperature for about two weeks. The roots develop during this time. The potted bulbs are then placed in 40°F storage for at least six weeks.

Late November—early December potting.—Bulbs for this potting time should be case-cooled in moist peat for six weeks before potting. There should be no delay between cooling and potting because warm temperatures may cancel the cooling effects. The potted bulbs are watered and placed in greenhouses at 65°F night temperature.

Forcing.—Forcing is started from mid- to late December, depending on the date of Easter and on the kind of cultivar. The first concern is root development. Bottom heating and allowing the soil to dry somewhat between irrigations favors root growth. Night temperature generally is 65°F for the first month, followed by 60°F night temperature until maturity. Higher temperatures hasten maturity, and lower temperatures delay it.

If it is possible that the fall cool treatment was not long enough, long photoperiods in the early stages of growth are suitable substitutes. As a safeguard, some lily growers provide long photoperiods for one week after shoot emergence.

Leaf counting or other means may be used to estimate the rate of development during the cropping period, and temperature adjustments are made accordingly.

If some plants mature too rapidly, they may be placed in refrigerators at 40°F until the time for marketing.

POINSETTIA

It is possible to produce poinsettia crops year-round, but this plant continues to be associated mainly with the Christmas season.

Types and Areas of Production

Poinsettia vary in several characteristics, like bract color, size, number, and shape; leaf shape and abscission; plant height; branching; and the length of time needed for flowering after the start of short photoperiods. The red-bract cultivars are grown in the greatest quantity. Leaf retention is considered desirable. The significance of the other characteristics depends on growers and uses.

Poinsettia may be grown either single-stem or branched, in pot sizes from 4 to 12 inches. They may also be grown in hanging baskets or as standard trees. Most poinsettia are grown in 6½-inch pots, either as one branched plant or as three single-stem plants. Poinsettia is a common pot-plant crop throughout the United States and Canada.

Crop-Starter Plants, Propagating, and Planting

Poinsettia are propagated from stem-tip cuttings. The cropping period may be from July to December, depending on the sizes of the mature plants. The plants in 12-inch pots, with a mature height of 3 feet, are planted in July. The plants for 6½-inch pots may be potted in mid-August. The plants for 4-inch pots may be potted in September.

Crop-starter plants may be purchased from specialist propagators.

Or pot-plant growers may start stock plants in May for production of cuttings in the summer and early fall. Some of these growers also produce additional rooted cuttings for sale to local growers.

Poinsettia may be propagated in benches, small pots, or blocks. When they are rooted, the rooted cuttings are potted as shallow as possible. The starter plants rooted in small pots or blocks should be potted at the same depth as they are in propagation pots or blocks. More than one starter plant may be used per pot, although only one plant is used per 4-inch pot. One or three plants are used per 6½-inch pot, depending on whether the plant(s) will be grown branched or single-stem. Accordingly greater numbers of starter plants are used with increases in pot sizes.

Temperature and Photoperiod

For stock plants, a night temperature of 70°F is used. A night temperature of 65°F may be used after potting until mid-October and then may be adjusted depending on the rate of plant growth and development.

Poinsettia flower in short photoperiods. — The natural daylength in fall is satisfactory for Christmas flowering of poinsettia, but for earlier-than-Christmas flowering, short photoperiods are provided by light exclusion. If there is electric lighting in the vicinity of poinsettia, light exclusion also has to be used for the Christmas crop. Poinsettia is sensitive to very low amounts of light.

Problems

Photoperiod lighting is used during spring and summer for stock plants to ensure that the photoperiods are long. Variable-length photoperiods for stock plants may produce plants with branched tips.

If plants in a greenhouse area do not develop flowers, this condition may be caused by stray electric light from either within or outside the greenhouse.

Disease can usually be avoided when pathogen-free starter plants are used, when soil is steamed before use, when starter plants are shallow-planted, and when soil is allowed to dry somewhat between irrigations.

MISCELLANEOUS POT PLANTS

The pot plants that are generally grown in smaller quantities are grouped here. Some of these pot plants are rather recent commercial introductions. Others will be added to greenhouse production. Information sources about plant introductions include trade periodicals, plant vendors, and Cooperative Extension Service bulletins.

African Violet

Pot-plant growers may start their African violet crops either by propagation by leaf or with starter plants purchased from specialists.

Cropping period.—African violet may be cropped year-round. The length of the cropping period, from the start of propagation to the mature 4-inch pot plant, is about nine months.

Fig. 7-10. African violet produced in a 4-inch pot.

The length of the cropping time from potting starter plant to mature 4-inch pot plant is about three months.

Light and temperature.—Sunlight has to be heavily shaded from spring to fall, but only light shade may be needed in winter. Movable shade allows suitable adjustment of the amount of light.

African violet can be grown very well solely in electric lighting. Fluorescent lamps are usually used so the plants receive 500 foot-candles of light for 16 hours daily.

A night temperature of 70°F is used.

Problems.—Cool water on leaves causes yellow spotting. The plants have to be shielded from drips. Unless irrigating with warm water, it is necessary to avoid depositing moisture on the leaves.

Fig. 7-11. Cold-water leaf spot on African violet.

Begonia, Hiemalis

Types.—These begonia have a wide assortment of flower colors in white, yellow, orange, red, and pink. Upright growers are used for pot plants and lateral growers for hanging baskets. Cultivars vary in susceptibility to powdery mildew.

Cropping period.—Hiemalis begonia may be cropped year-round, but the best season is spring. The length of crop time is about 12 to 14 weeks. The crop-starter plants are small pot plants, propagated by leaf or stem tip, by specialists who maintain pathogen-free stock.

Temperature and photoperiod.—In the early stages of growth, 71°F night temperature and long photoperiods are used. For long photoperiods in naturally short days, lighting is provided to extend the day.

For flowering, 63°F night temperature and short photoperiods are used.

Problems.—Powdery mildew, bacterial blight, and botrytis rot diseases are possible in moist conditions.

Cultivars that are not susceptible to powdery mildew should be used, and pathogen-free crop-starter plants should be purchased. Surroundings should be adjusted so the plant surfaces are dry.

Bulbs

The most common crops started from bulbs are crocus, daffodil, hyacinth, and tulip. Short-growing cultivars of daffodil and tulip are used.

For early-season flowering, temperature-treated (precooled) bulbs are used. For later flowering, regular (nonprecooled) bulbs are used.

Cropping period.—For crocus flowering from mid-December to

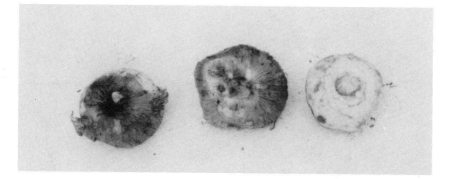

Fig. 7-12. Crocus corms. At left, topside; at center, bottom side; at right, topside with skin removed.

Fig. 7-13. Hyacinth bulbs. At left, topside; at center, bottom side; at right, dark-flowered cultivars also have dark bulbs.

mid-January, precooled corms are planted during the first week in October. For flowering from late January to late February, regular corms are planted from late September to late October.

For daffodil flowering from late December to mid-January, precooled bulbs are planted during the first week in October. For flowering from late January to late April, regular bulbs are planted from late September to mid-November.

For hyacinth flowering from late December to mid-January, prepared bulbs are planted from mid- to late September. For flowering from late January to April, regular bulbs are planted from late September to mid-November.

Fig. 7-14. Tulip bulbs. At left, two with skin intact, both top and bottom; at right, two with skin removed, both top and bottom.

For tulip flowering from early January to early February, precooled bulbs are planted during the first two weeks in October. For flowering from mid-February to early May, regular bulbs are planted from the first week in October to mid-November.

Planting and refrigerating temperature.—All of the bulbs are planted with the upper tips just above the soil surface. The skin is removed from tulip before planting, and the bulb is planted with the flat side toward the edge of the pot because the first leaf develops on that side of the bulb.

Refrigerating temperatures are 48°F for several weeks and then 41°F until the first week in January. The bulbs remaining in storage from mid-January on are supplied with a 35°F temperature.

Forcing temperature and time.—Crocus forcing requires about 10 days, either with 60°F night temperatures for early forcing or with 55°F night temperatures for later forcing.

Daffodil are not brought in for forcing until the flower bud can be felt in the bulb neck. Forcing temperature is 60°F at night. Early forcing requires about three weeks, and later forcing requires one week.

Early hyacinth forcing requires 73°F night temperatures for about 10 days, followed by 65°F night temperatures. The forcing time is about three weeks. Midseason forcing requires 65°F night temperatures for two weeks. Late-season forcing requires 60°F night temperatures for about one week.

Tulip early-season forcing requires 65°F night temperatures for about five weeks. Late forcing requires 60°F night temperatures for about three weeks.

Cineraria

Cropping period and areas of production.—Cineraria is a late-winter—early-spring crop that is started from seed sown from August to November. It is a cool-climate crop that is satisfactory in the northern United States and Canada.

Temperature.—The seedlings are grown at 60°F night temperature for about two months. Flower development requires six weeks in temperatures of 55°F or less. The plants are mature and ready for marketing after another two months at 55° to 60°F night temperature.

Cyclamen

Cropping period and crop-starter plants.—With fast-crop methods, the length of the cropping period for cyclamen in 6½-inch pots may be about 10 months from seed or about 7 months if seedlings in small pots are used for crop starters. For cyclamen in 4-inch pots, the length of the cropping period is about eight months from seed and about five months from seedlings in small pots.

Cyclamen is a cool-climate crop, generally flowering from December to March.

Temperature.—The required temperature is 68°F for the propagation and early growth of seedlings. After potting, the required temperature is 62°F at night.

Some particulars.—Cyclamen seed is large and individually sown. Sometimes the seed is sown in packs that are large enough for seedling growth.

Fig. 7-15. Small cyclamen plant with globular stem in view at soil surface.

The stem at soil surface is globe shape. To avoid disease, the top of the globe must be left above the soil surface in repotting the plant.

Gibberellic acid sprays may be used at the 10-leaf stage to promote flowering.

Exacum

Cropping period and crop-starter plants.—Exacum may be grown year-round, but it is generally more satisfactory for flowering spring to fall.

Exacum is started from seed. However, because of some propagation and small-plant problems, pot-plant growers often start their crops with small plants purchased from specialists. The length of the cropping period is about two months for plants flowered from spring to fall.

Light and temperature.—Some shading of summer sunlight is needed. A night temperature of 62°F may be used.

Problems.—Exacum is subject to some types of rot in moist surroundings.

Geranium

The three types of geranium grown from cuttings are known as *zonal, ivy,* and *regal.*

The zonal geranium is mainly produced in 4-inch pots that are widely used in gardening and landscaping.

Ivy geranium is mainly used in hanging baskets and outdoor window planters because they have trailing type growth.

Regal geranium is generally used for spring house plants in 6½-inch pots.

Crop-starters.—Stem-tip cuttings are used for propagating. Geranium growers purchase pathogen-free rooted cuttings or small pot plants for starting either stock plants or 4-inch crops. Stock plants for zonal geranium cutting production are planted in 7- or 8-inch pots about three months before the cutting harvest. Unrooted cuttings are commonly stuck directly in the 4-inch pots. The length of the cropping period is about two months from the sticking of the cutting to the marketing of the mature plant.

If stock plants are used for ivy geranium, they may be planted in hanging baskets instead of pots and started about one month earlier than for zonal geranium stock plants. The hanging baskets are planted with rooted cuttings or with plants in small pots about three months before marketing.

Crop-starter plants for regal geranium are purchased from geranium specialists and planted directly in 6½-inch pots.

Light and temperature.—Generally, the full amount of sunlight is provided for geranium, and 60°F night temperature is used.

Problems.—Many geranium diseases can be avoided by the use of pathogen-free crop starters and steamed soil.

If plant surfaces remain moist and if humidity remains high, edema and botrytis rot may occur. Ivy geranium are particularly susceptible to edema.

Gloxinia

Pot-plant growers usually start gloxinia crops from seedlings in small pots purchased from specialist growers. Gloxinia can be a year-round crop, but more commonly it is a spring and summer crop. At 65°F night temperature, the length of time from potting to marketing in 6½-inch pots is from 10 to 12 weeks.

For spring-summer cropping, gloxinia require shading from sunlight.

Hydrangea

Crop-starters and cropping period.—Hydrangea are propagated from stem-tip or stem-segment cuttings. Because of the difficulties in maintaining stock plants as a source of cuttings, pot-plant growers either purchase unrooted cuttings from hydrangea specialists in the spring, or they purchase dormant budded plants in the fall.

Rooted cuttings are usually potted in May, and during the summer the plants may be grown in greenhouses or outdoors. Flower buds are well developed in October, and the plants are placed in cool storage until the time for forcing. Easter is the main marketing period for hydrangea, and forcing starts in late December to early January, depend-

Fig. 7-16. Hydrangea pot plant to be marketed.

ing on the date of Easter. That cropping period is about 11 months long.

If the crop is started with dormant budded plants, the plants may be received in October, repotted, and placed in cool storage. This is a cropping period of about six months. Sometimes dormant budded plants are received in December after they have had their cool treatment. Those plants can then be repotted and placed in greenhouses for forcing.

Hydrangea is a cool-climate crop, and it requires frequent irrigation during hot weather.

Summer and early fall growing.—The main production in the summer and early fall is of two- and three-branched plants in 6½-inch pots. The plants are pinched in early July to cause branching.

Hydrangea flower color depends on the available aluminum in the plants—the flowers are pink without aluminum and blue with it. Generally, the flowers will be pink when the soil is above pH 6 and phosphorus fertilizers are also used, and the flowers will be blue when the soil is below pH 6 and phosphorus fertilizers are not used. In addition, the plants that are scheduled to be blue flowers are supplied with some aluminum fertilizers during the summer as well as during forcing.

By October, the flower buds should be visible in the stem tips.

Fall cool period.—For prompt flowering during forcing, the plants have to be in temperatures below 50°F for at least six weeks. Dark storage is used in sheds or refrigerators. The leaves drop during storage.

Bud rot can be a problem in storage because of the moist surroundings.

Forcing.—The length of forcing is about 13 weeks at 60°F night temperature.

When the plants are brought in, the first consideration is new root growth. Allowing the soil to dry somewhat between irrigations and using bottom heating are satisfactory for root growth.

Kalanchoe

Kalanchoe crops are generally started from plants in small pots that are purchased from specialists. Flowering occurs in short photoperiods. Because kalanchoe are sensitive to light and to high temperatures, fall-to-spring crops may be more successful than spring-to-fall crops. The length of crop time is about 13 weeks in 4-inch pots and about 16 weeks in 6½-inch pots.

Night temperatures are 68°F during long photoperiods and 63°F during the short photoperiod time to maturity. The length of time during long photoperiods is about one week for plants in 4-inch pots and four weeks for plants in 6½-inch pots. All stems of the plants are pinched at about the time short photoperiods begin.

Lily, Colored

There are many variables with colored lily cultivars, like flower color, size, number, and out- or up-facing blossoms; length of time to flowering; mature plant height; leaf characteristics; susceptibility to disease; and effects of growth regulators. Growers need colored-lily bulb vendors who have reliable bulbs and information.

Precooling.—Usually the bulbs are vendor-cooled at 35°F for at least six weeks, then frozen at 28°F. The bulbs are shipped from vendor to grower at forcing time.

Cropping period.—The length of forcing time may be from 65 to 100 days, depending on the cultivar, the temperature, and the season of the year. Although colored lily may be forced whenever bulbs are available, spring forcing is common.

Summer temperatures may be too high for the forcing of some colored lily plants.

Forcing.—Night temperatures from 50° to 60°F may be used for forcing, but the temperature and length of cropping time information should be supplied by the vendor for each cultivar.

Vendors should also supply information about growth regulator use for each cultivar.

Chapter 8

CAREERS

In greenhouse flower and plant businesses, there may be careers for associates, managers, a general manager, and advisors. While managers are responsible for the operation of a specific unit of the business, the general manager oversees the entire organization. In larger firms, associates may be assigned to one phase of the operation; however, in smaller companies they may be expected to fill in whenever they are needed.

Because of differences in activities and types of work, the units of a business are producing, marketing, maintaining, and watching after-hours.

Pay for the various careers in greenhouse businesses is competitive with that of positions with comparable responsibility in other industries. Fringe benefits that are offered usually are similar to the benefits provided by other firms.

Advisors are not employed by greenhouse businesses but because of the close relationships between greenhouse management and vendor representatives and/or extension service specialists, comments about the careers of these advisors are included here.

ASSOCIATE

Many businesses need both independent and dependent associates.

The independents, because of schooling or work experience, know the work basics and are capable of independently doing assigned tasks.

Type of Work

The type of work may be in producing, marketing, maintaining, and watching after-hours. General managers and managers expect that graduates of vocational schools and applicants with work experience will know the following basics:

Producing

Knowing plants and how they grow
Preparing soil for planting
Planting various types of crops
Pinching
Irrigating
Regulating heating, cooling, and ventilating
Applying fertilizer
Recognizing pest and pathogen symptoms
Harvesting
Doing pipe-fitting
Preparing plants and flowers for marketing

Marketing

Knowing plants and plant growth
Regulating temperature, moisture, and light for flowers and
    plants
Receiving shipments
Designing flowers and plants
Displaying flowers, plants, and supplies
Selling by customer visit and telephone
Writing sales slips
Making computer entries
Preparing plants and flowers for shipping

Improving appearance of self, sales area, and delivery

Delivering

Maintaining

Using hand tools

Fitting pipe

Using greenhouse buildings and equipment

Measuring, squaring, and leveling

Watching after-hours

Using greenhouse buildings and equipment

Adjusting temperature and heat distribution

Ventilating

Generating emergency electric service

Hours of Work

Working hours may vary within an organization according to the duties to be performed as well as from one company to another. Usually overtime is necessary before holidays and special-event sales.

Most businesses are closed for Thanksgiving, Christmas, New Year's Day, Memorial Day, the Fourth of July, and Labor Day.

Typical hours for different divisions are listed below:

Producing—Greenhouse hours: 8:00 a.m. to 4:30 p.m. Monday through Friday with a half hour for lunch, and 8:00 a.m. to noon on Saturday.

Associates in rose greenhouses rotate for harvesting flowers on weekends and holidays.

Marketing—Wholesale store hours: 6:00 a.m. to 4:00 p.m. Monday through Friday and 8:00 a.m. to noon on Saturday.

Route salespeople depart early enough to arrive at the first stop at the customer's opening time. They may return to the wholestore about midafternoon.

Wholesale shippers hours vary with product availability, destination of shipment, and method of shipping.

Retail flower shop hours, which vary with the location, generally are the same as others in the vicinity—9:00 a.m. to 5:00 p.m. among offices and other stores and 10:00 a.m. to 9:00 p.m. in mall. Associates may be scheduled for 40-hour weeks plus additional time during holiday and special-event marketing.

Interiorscape office hours: 9:00 a.m. to 5:00 p.m., but associates usually must be scheduled for whenever planting and maintenance can be done at customers' sites.

Maintaining—Scheduled hours: 8:00 a.m. to 4:30 p.m. Monday through Friday and 8:00 a.m. to noon on Saturday, but staff may be subject to call at any time during emergencies.

Watching after-hours—Hours vary with the season of the year, type of crop, extent of automatic controls, and general manager's preferences.

Pay

Entry-level pay for dependent associates can be expected to be federal minimum wage; pay for independents would be greater because of the amount of schooling and work experience. At the time of the employment interview the starting wage, intervals between job evaluations, and the possible maximum wage should be discussed.

Pay usually is figured on the hourly rate times the number of hours worked, but some salespeople are paid a base pay plus a percent of sales above established sales levels.

MANAGER

Depending on the size of the business, there may be one or more managers in producing, marketing, and maintaining. During the hiring interview, the general manager assigns responsibility and grants authority to the new staff member.

Not only must managers be very familiar with all of the basics listed earlier for associates, but also because of schooling and work experience, they must have an in-depth knowledge of their field.

Some of the responsibilities of managers are:

Hiring, training, assigning, promoting, and releasing associates

Communicating effectively with associates, other managers, and the general manager

Making projections and plans

Adjusting own working hours to job needs

Being flexible and adaptable to changing situations

Scheduling work by priorities

Checking results

Analyzing work on the basis of comparing sales and expenses

Some specific responsibilities by area of management are:

Producing

Identifying market needs

Planning crops to meet those needs

Making rotations that use available space and satisfy market needs

Purchasing necessary crop starters, supplies, and equipment

Planning timing of planting, pinching, irrigating, and harvesting

Adjusting light, heat, ventilation, and fertilizer

Evaluating plant growth and development continuously for scheduled maturity dates

Marketing

When greenhouse operators establish their own wholesale stores, wholesale shipping organizations, or retail flower shops, these marketing units usually need managers. Manager responsibilities vary with the type of marketing unit.

Wholesale store—Managers are responsible for:

Locating customers and evaluating their needs

Locating suppliers of flowers and plants as needed in addition to own greenhouse production

Keeping reliable suppliers who ship fresh flowers and plants of needed quality and quantity at scheduled times

Placing advance orders based on the past year's business and knowing what flowers and plants are available for immediate shipments

Using telephone and fax to keep informed of worldwide flower and plant availability and quantity

Making computer entries for purchasing, sales, and inventory

Purchasing, warehousing, displaying, and selling florists' supplies

Hiring, training, assigning, promoting, and releasing sales and delivery people

Attending local and state association industry meetings

Attending national florists' supplies meetings and trade shows

Collecting accounts receivable

Wholesale shipper—There are various types of shipping organizations but managers generally are involved in:

Locating customers and evaluating their needs

Locating suppliers of flowers and plants as needed in addition to their own greenhouse production

Visiting suppliers often enough to be continuously informed of quality and quantity

Hiring, training, assigning, promoting, and releasing salespeople, packers, and deliverers

Collecting accounts receivable

Flower shop—Managers usually design and sell and are otherwise involved in:

Locating customers and evaluating their needs

Planning advertising

Buying flowers and plants as needed in addition to their own greenhouse production

Buying supplies

Hiring, training, assigning, promoting, and releasing designers, salespeople, and deliverers

Attending local and state association industry meetings

Collecting accounts receivable

Maintaining

The managers, within the capabilities of their people and equipment, maintain buildings and equipment, do minor construction, and operate some power equipment and machines. The type jobs that are handled may be:

Laying out beds, benches, and walks in greenhouses
Constructing benches and walks
Operating heat generators
Installing soil drainage pipe
Maintaining the water source
Maintaining the ventilating equipment
Fitting pipe for water and heating systems
Repairing and replacing greenhouse covering
Painting buildings
Scheduling vehicle maintenance
Maintaining carts and conveyors
Maintaining emergency electric generation
Handling soil

GENERAL MANAGER

The general manager is responsible for the conduct of the entire business. In family businesses, the general manager often is the member who controls the major number of shares of stock in the corporation.

General managers may work in various parts of the business, and in addition, they establish operating policies, generate and allocate funds for capital investments and operating expenses, make decisions about capital investments, analyze business results, and arrange for transfer of general management.

Establishing operating policies—Some of the business policies set by general managers are:

> Responsibilities to employees and community
>
> Responsibilities of employees to company
>
> Formulas for wages, salaries, and fringe benefits
>
> Type of customers to be served
>
> Responsibilities to customers
>
> Business hours, working hours, and time off
>
> How customer credit may be established
>
> Methods of payment of payroll and accounts payable
>
> Procedures for collection of accounts receivable
>
> Relationship and communication among members of the company
>
> Theft control

Generating funds—General managers or owners cause funds to be generated by:

> Long-term loans for capital investment in the company
>
> Line-of-credit loans for operating expenses
>
> Controlling expense and sales for satisfactory cash flow
>
> Collecting accounts receivable
>
> Preventing loss of assets

Making decisions about capital investments—The capital investments may be:

> Purchasing land
>
> Improving land grade and drainage
>
> Purchasing buildings
>
> Purchasing costly equipment
>
> Making extensive repairs
>
> Providing a water source

Providing some utilities

Developing some fuel sources

Analyzing business results—Results of business may be analyzed by:

Establishing chart of accounts that allows valid comparisons of sales and expenses

Developing monthly year-to-date income statements and balance sheets for current and past year

Determining causes for results

Arranging for transfer of general management—Because companies can and should be timeless and general managers are necessarily transitory, general managers have to allow for the continuous well-being of the company by a carefully planned transfer of general management.

ADVISOR

Vendor representatives and Cooperative Extension Service specialists are advisors for greenhouse flower and plant businesses.

Vendor Representatives

Careers with vendors may be in the firms' headquarters or as traveling salespeople. Vendor specialists and salespeople often have four-year or advanced degrees plus work experience.

The headquarters specialists may be in telephone sales, purchasing, writing, producing, and shipping. Many of these people work regular office hours and five-day weeks. Pay may be salary based on responsibilities.

Traveling salespeople have irregular hours based on making schedules and reports for customers; travel time to customers; customer visits; and local, state, and national conventions. Pay may be base salary plus commissions on sales.

Vendor services include:

Publishing catalogs that describe plants and supplies and how they are used

Publishing periodicals containing current information

Offering information by telephone and visitation

Scheduling some crops

Extending long-term credit and advice on funding

Cooperative Extension Service Specialists

Careers with the Cooperative Extension Service may be at federal, state, province, and county locations. The specialists who deal with greenhouse flower and plant matters usually are at state and province locations. The areas of specialty are plant physiology, entomology, plant pathology, marketing, economics, and engineering. The specialists usually have Ph. D. degrees. Extension specialists may have split assignments in extension and research.

The Cooperative Extension Service is operated with federal and state or province funds. The Cooperative Extension Service Specialists provide aid in their various areas of specialization by:

Conducting meetings at state, province, and county locations

Participating in industry meetings

Publishing bulletins

Conducting training sessions

Holding conferences at extension or business locations

GLOSSARY

ABSCISSION – Leaf drop from plants.

ACIDITY – A pH value less than 7.

AERATED – Supplied with air.

AEROSOL – A means of dispensing pesticides from pressurized containers.

ALKALINITY – A pH value greater than 7.

BAY – A structural division of a greenhouse.

BED – A ground area where cut-flower plants or pot plants are grown.

BENCH – A constructed area where cut-flower plants or pot plants are grown.

BISEXUAL – A flower that contains both male and female parts.

BLIND SHOOTS – Rose stems that do not terminate with flowers.

BOILER – A heat generator for steam or hot-water heating systems.

BRACT – A modified leaf immediately below the flowers of some plants, like the red bracts of poinsettia.

BRANCH – A lateral shoot; to produce lateral shoots.

BUD – The origin of a shoot or flower.

BULB – A globular underground stem that has a terminal bud.

BUNCH – Cut flowers of the same kind and quality, wrapped in marketable units.

BUSHY – The appearance of plants that have plentiful branching.

CHLOROPHYLL – The green pigment in plants.

CHLOROSIS – Yellowing of leaves, caused by lack of chlorophyll.

COMPOUND LEAF – A leaf with its blade divided into leaflets.

CONDENSATE – The water formed from condensation of steam in heating pipelines.

CONSUMERS – Those who buy products for their own uses.

CORM – A globular underground stem that has terminal and lateral buds.

COUPLING – A fitting used to join pipe or hose together.

CROP – The plants or flowers being grown or harvested.

CROP-STARTER – The plant or plant part used for starting crops.

CULTIVAR – A crop plant.

CUSTOMERS – Those who buy products but not necessarily for their own uses.

CUT – To harvest flowers.

CUT-BACK – A severe pruning of the entire top part of cut-flower plants to reduce the height of the plants.

CUT FLOWER – A flower that is harvested and sold.

CUTTING – A vegetative part of a plant, used for propagation.

CYMOSE – A determinate-type flower cluster. The topmost or inner florets develop first.

DAMPING-OFF – Common term for rot diseases at the lower stem of seedlings.

DIBBLE – A pencil-shaped tool used for planting seedlings.

DIRECT PLANTING – Planting rooted cuttings or seedlings directly in crop benches or pots.

DISBUD – To remove flower buds for improvement of flowering.

DISEASE ORGANISM – A fungus, bacterium, or virus that can cause disease.

DORMANT – Not in an active stage of growth.

DRAINAGE – The movement of water through or away from the soil.

EAVE – The place where a building sidewall joins the roof.

ELL – A fitting that is used for any change in the direction of pipelines.

ENERGY – A force or power that is able to do work.

ENVIRONMENT – The immediate or effective surroundings.

EXHAUST FAN – A fan that is used to remove air from greenhouses for ventilating or cooling.

EYE – A vegetative bud at a node.

FAN – A mechanical means of moving air in greenhouses.

FAN AND PAD COOLING – A method of reducing air temperature in greenhouses by exhausting the internal air with fans and allowing the external air to enter through moistened pads.

FEMALE FLOWER – A unisexual flower that has only female sexual parts. A female flower may also be called a pistillate flower.

FEMALE THREADS – Internal threads, such as those found in pipe fittings.

FERTILIZER – A source of necessary minerals for plants.

F₁ HYBRID – The seed that results from cross-pollinating suitable pure-line parent plants.

FLAT – A tray or box, about 15 inches by 20 inches by 3 inches in dimension, that is used for carrying pot plants.

FLORET – An individual flower of a flower cluster.

FLORICULTURE – The producing and marketing of ornamental plants and flowers.

FLOWER – The sexually reproductive part of a plant. A flower may be male, female, or bisexual.

FLOWER CLUSTER – A type of flowering that has more than one flower or floret per stem.

FLOWER STEM – A stem that has one or more flowers.

FOLIAGE – Leaves.

FOOT-CANDLE – A unit for measuring illumination.

FORCE – To provide suitable conditions for plant growth.

FUNGICIDE – A material used to control or eradicate fungus pathogens.

GEOTROPISM – The direction of plant growth resulting from gravity.

GERMINATION – The start of growth in seed.

GRADING – Grouping or sorting plants and flowers of the same size and quality into marketable units.

GRAFT – Vegetative propagation by the joining of a stem part from the plant being reproduced to another plant.

GROW ON – To continue growth of a plant to a larger, more mature size.

GROWTH SUBSTANCE – A material that regulates the amount or kind of plant growth.

GUTTER – A trough installed to conduct rain water from the roofs of joined greenhouses.

HARDEN – To place vased cut flowers in cool temperatures during marketing.

HEAT – The form of energy that causes an increase in temperature when it is added and a decrease in temperature when it is removed.

HEATING PIPELINES – A means of distributing heat in greenhouses.

HOLD – To keep plants or flowers in conditions that limit further growth and maturity.

HORMONE – A growth substance that influences the growth and development of plants.

HORTICULTURE – The producing and marketing of ornamental plants, fruits, or vegetables.

HUMIDITY – The amount of moisture in the air in terms of the percent of total amount of moisture that the air could contain.

HYBRIDIZATION – The formation of new cultivars by the cross-pollination of plants of different genetic characters.

INFLORESCENCE – A flower cluster.

INORGANIC MATTER – Material that is not living or did not originate from a living individual.

INSECTICIDE – A material used for the control or eradication of insects.

INTERNODE – The stem part between nodes.

IRRIGATING – Supplying water to soil.

LATERAL FLOWER – A flower that occurs at a node below the stem tip.

LATERAL SHOOTS – A shoot that occurs at a node below the stem tip.

LEACH – To apply large quantities of water to the soil at one time to reduce the amount of fertilizer in the soil.

LIFT – To harvest rooted cuttings from propagation soil.

MALE FLOWER – A unisexual flower that contains only male sexual parts.

MALE THREADS – External threads, such as those on pipe.

MATURE – Fully grown, or at a marketable stage of development.

MINERAL – Inorganic material.

MUM – An abbreviation of chrysanthemum.

MUTATION – A heritable change in a vegetative part of a plant.

NETWORK – A means of supporting plant stems for upright growth.

NODE – A location in stems where leaves and shoots may develop.

ORGANIC MATTER – Plants or animals or their refuse.

PATHOGEN – An organism that can cause disease.

PEAT MOSS – Partly decayed sphagnum moss that is used in soil mixtures.

PEDUNCLE – A stem that has a flower or flowers.

PESTICIDE – A material used for the control or eradication of pests.

PESTS – Generally, insects and mites.

PETAL – Frequently, the showy part of a flower.

PETIOLE – A leaf stalk.

pH – A symbol that expresses acidity or alkalinity. The pH 7 indicates neutrality. Acidity increase is indicated by decreases in numbers below pH 7, and alkalinity increase is indicated by increases in numbers above pH 7.

PHOTOPERIOD – The daily duration of light.

PHOTOSYNTHESIS – The manufacture of sugar in plants.

PHOTOTROPISM – The type of plant growth caused by one-sided illumination.

PIGMENT – A substance that is commonly identified by the color of light it reflects.

PINCH – To remove a stem tip.

PIPE FITTINGS – Various attachments used for joining pipes.

PISTIL – The female part of a plant.

POLLEN – Dust-size particles that transfer from stamen to pistil during pollination.

POT-TO-POT – Pot plants that are set so the pots are next to each other.

PPM – Parts per million; a common means of expressing the amount of material in a solution or mixture.

PRICK-OFF – To transplant seedlings from seed flats to pots or to other containers.

PROPAGATION – Reproduction of plants.

PRUNE – To remove some stems to improve the growth or appearance of plants.

PURLINS – Roof framework members that are lengthwise and spaced equidistant between the ridge and the eave or gutter.

RACEMOSE – An indeterminate flower cluster. The topmost or inner florets continue to develop, or they develop last.

REPRODUCTION – The propagation or multiplication of the same cultivar.

REPRODUCTIVE – A type of plant development leading to the production of flowers.

RESPIRATION – The oxidation of food within plants.

RETAILING – Marketing directly to consumers.

RHIZOME – A leafless stem that grows horizontally, usually just below the soil surface.

RIDGE – The top-center framework member of a greenhouse.

ROTATION – The crop succession producing the kinds and amounts of crops when needed and fully using greenhouse space.

SEEDLING – The plant that develops from seed.

SEPAL – The flower part just below the petals—sometimes the showy part of a flower.

SEXUAL PROPAGATION – The reproduction of plants by seed.

SHOOT – A young stem.

SHORT DAY – A photoperiod that is short.

SINGLE-STEM – A plant that is grown so only one flowering stem is produced.

SLEEVE – A paper or plastic-film cone placed around a plant for its protection during shipping.

SOIL – Any material in which roots grow.

SOIL TEST – To determine the drainage and fertilizer status of soil.

SOLUBLE SALTS – The total supply of soil minerals that is available to plants.

SPLITTING – A malformation of the flower in poinsettia or carnation.

STAMEN – The male part of a plant.

STEAMING – The process of using steam to eliminate pathogens, pests, and weeds from soils.

STICK – To place unrooted cuttings in propagating soil for rooting to occur.

STOCK PLANT – A plant that is used as a source of cuttings for propagation.

STOMATES – Pores in plant surfaces which, when open, allow exchange of gases between plants and surroundings.

TEMPERATURE – The amount of hotness or coldness.

TERMINAL FLOWER – The flower that develops in the stem tip of a plant.

THERMOMETER – A sensing device that indicates temperature.

THERMOSTAT – A sensing device that makes electrical contact at a set temperature.

TRANSPIRATION – The loss of water vapor from plant tissues to surroundings.

TRAP – A steam trap that allows water but not steam to pass through.

TRUSS – A framework member that supports the roof without the use of interior posts.

TUBER – A type of root or underground stem. Tubers are usually oval-shaped. Root tubers have stem development only at one end. Stem tubers are underground stems with nodes spaced somewhat equidistantly.

UNION – Pipe fittings that connect pipes but that can be separated for repair of pipes or installation of equipment.

UNISEXUAL – Flowers that have either male or female parts but not both.

VARIEGATED – Plant parts that have more than one color.

VASE – A container used for placing cut-flower stems in water.

VEGETATIVE – A type of stem growth that develops stem and leaves.

VEGETATIVE PROPAGATION – The reproduction of plants by plant parts other than seed.

VENTILATOR – A roof or wall section that is hinged from the ridge or eave and that can be opened for ventilation.

WATERLOGGED SOIL – Soil that is water-saturated because of insufficient drainage.

WATER VAPOR – The gaseous form of water.

WHOLESALING – Marketing to wholesalers or retailers.

QUESTIONS FOR CHAPTERS AND FOR INDEXED SUBJECTS

Questions for Chapters

Chapter 1. Flower and Plant Producing and Marketing

1. What kinds of flowers and plants are generally grown in U.S. and Canadian greenhouses?
2. Why aren't all types of flowers and pot plants grown in greenhouses throughout the United States and Canada?
3. What are some differences between wholesale and retail marketing?
4. What kinds of jobs are there in greenhouse businesses?
5. In addition to schooling, how can more information be obtained about flower and plant production greenhouses?

Chapter 2. Plants

1. What are some ways greenhouse plants differ from animals?
2. What are nodes?
3. What parts of plants are underground?
4. What are the differences between solitary and cluster flowers?

5. What is a bisexual flower?

6. What is a unisexual flower?

7. What are the names for the showy parts of flowers?

8. What are the differences between flowers and florets?

9. What are the differences between terminal and lateral flowers?

10. Do stems and roots grow from the bases or from the tips?

11. How do plants get food?

12. How is food used by plants?

13. How does moisture enter plants?

14. How does moisture exit plants?

15. How does light enter plants?

16. What happens to light that enters plants?

17. How does carbon dioxide enter plants?

18. How do minerals enter plants?

19. How does light affect plant growth?

20. How does heat affect plant growth?

21. How does moisture affect plant growth?

22. How do minerals affect plant growth?

Chapter 3. Buildings and Equipment

1. What is a greenhouse?

2. How are greenhouses built to allow for the entry of the maximum amount of sunlight?

3. Can electric lighting be used for growing plants? Explain.

4. What sources of heat are used for greenhouse plants?

5. How is heat distributed in greenhouses?

6. What provisions are there for the removal of heat from greenhouses?

7. Where are greenhouse ventilators located?

8. If a greenhouse has a fan and tube ventilation system, where are the fans and tubes located?

9. Where are the fans and pad located in a fan and pad cooling system?

10. What sources of water are used for greenhouse businesses?

11. How is water distributed in greenhouses?

12. How is water removed from greenhouses?

13. What kinds of equipment do greenhouse businesses have?

Chapter 4. Adjusting Plant Surroundings

1. What plant surroundings may need adjustment?

2. Does adjustment of a single surrounding have any effects on the other surroundings? Explain.

3. How does air circulation affect plant growth?

Chapter 5. Working with Plants

1. What kinds of surroundings are needed for plant propagation?

2. What are the sources of plant materials for plant propagation?

3. Why is vegetative propagation used?

4. How are greenhouse soils prepared for planting?

5. How are plants planted?

6. Why does the soil surface need to be level after planting?

7. What work follows planting?

8. Why are plants pinched?

9. How are plants pinched?

10. How is plant growth regulated?

11. What is disbudding?

12. What is pruning?

13. Why are pot plants moved during crop production?

14. How are cut-flower plants provided enough space for mature plants?

15. Why is it necessary to be able to recognize pests?

16. What methods can be used to avoid disease?

Chapter 6. Cut-Flower Crops

1. What time of the year may daffodil and iris cut-flower crops be produced?

2. When are carnation crop plants started?

3. Why and when are carnation plants pinched?

4. When does carnation flower harvest start?

5. What types of carnation are grown?

6. What types of chrysanthemum are grown for cut flowers?

7. When are chrysanthemum flower crops produced?

8. Are chrysanthemum plants for cut-flower production pinched? Explain.

9. Why is it sometimes necessary to use either daily lighting or daily light exclusion for chrysanthemum crops?

10. How are rose flower crops started?

11. Why are rose plants pinched?

12. In harvesting, why is the position of the cut on rose stems important?

Chapter 7. Pot-Plant Crops

1. What is the natural cropping season for azalea?

2. What kinds of natural-season azalea crop-starters are used?

3. Why are azalea sheared?

4. Is it possible for local growers to have azalea crops for year-round sale? Explain.

5. What types of chrysanthemum are used for pot-plant production?

6. What kinds of crop starters are used for chrysanthemum pot plants?

7. Why do pot-plant growers purchase chrysanthemum cuttings from specialists rather than produce their own cuttings?

8. Why are chrysanthemum pot plants supplied some long photoperiods before the start of short days?

9. What methods are used to produce bushy 6-inch garden mums?

10. How much time is needed to produce a pot-mum crop?

11. Why are pot-mum plants disbudded?

12. Where are the main areas for foliage-plant production in the United States and Canada?

13. How do pot-plant growers use small foliage plants?

14. What general procedures do pot-plant growers use with medium and large foliage plants?

15. What is the main means of garden-plant propagation?

16. What kinds of specialization are there in garden-plant production?

17. In what ways are Easter lily crops started?

18. Why are Easter lily bulbs placed in temperatures below 50°F for at least six weeks before the start of forcing?

19. What can be done to hasten flowering if it appears that the Easter lily crops will be late for Easter?

20. What can be done with the Easter lily plants that mature too rapidly?

21. What type of crop starter is used for poinsettia pot plants?

22. When are poinsettia pot-plant crops started?

23. Why are photoperiodic lighting and shading used for poinsettia crops?

24. When do pot-plant growers who are going to propagate their own poinsettia crop starters start the stock plants?

25. How long does poinsettia propagation continue?

26. What are the production differences between large and small poinsettia pot plants?

27. How is African violet propagated?

28. When are African violet crops produced?

29. When may hiemalis begonia crops be produced?

30. What types of crop starters are used for hiemalis begonia?

31. What temperatures are used for bulb crops?

32. What are the main flowering periods for bulb crops?

33. How is cineraria propagated?

34. In what area of North America can cineraria be grown?

35. What is the marketing period for cineraria?

36. What temperatures do cineraria need?

37. How is cyclamen propagated?

38. What is the main marketing period for cyclamen?

39. How is exacum propagated?

40. What is the main marketing period for exacum?

41. What types of geranium pot plants are produced in greenhouses?

42. How are gloxinia pot-crops started, and what is the marketing period?

43. How are hydrangea pot plants propagated?

44. What is the marketing period for hydrangea?

45. What is the length of the cropping period for hydrangea?

46. Why are hydrangea placed in cool temperatures in the fall?

47. For kalanchoe in 6½-inch pots to be in flower in January, when would the crop need to be started?

48. How are kalanchoe pot-plant crops started?

Chapter 8. Careers

1. What kinds of work units are there in greenhouse businesses?

2. What kinds of information are needed for a productive associate position in greenhouse businesses?

3. What kinds of information are needed for a marketing associate position in greenhouse businesses?

4. What kinds of information do maintenance associates need for positions in greenhouse businesses?

5. What are the usual hours of work for production associates?

6. What are the usual hours of work for marketing associates?

7. In production greenhouses, how do associates' and managers' jobs differ?

8. In greenhouse businesses, how do managers' and general managers' jobs differ?

9. In what ways do venders advise greenhouse operators?

10. In what ways do Cooperative Extension Service people advise greenhouse operators?

Questions for Indexed Subjects

Air

1. Why do plants need carbon dioxide?

2. From what part of the surroundings do plants get carbon dioxide?

3. How do greenhouse operators maintain enough carbon dioxide for the plants?

4. Why do plants need oxygen?

5. What are some causes of air pollution in greenhouses?

6. What causes air to circulate?

7. What may happen if there is too much air circulation in greenhouses?

8. What causes greenhouse plants and surroundings to become too warm?

9. What causes outdoor air to be cooled as it goes through the moistened pad in a fan and pad system?

10. Is there air in soil? Explain.

11. What terms are used for air water?

12. What components and conditions of outdoor air are adjusted in greenhouses?

13. Is greenhouse air the same as outdoor air? Explain.

14. How do climate and geographical location affect the amount of air adjustment needed in greenhouses?

15. How are the components of air distributed uniformly throughout greenhouses?

16. What are the relationships between the following greenhouse air components and events: Continuously closed greenhouses and carbon dioxide? Well-ventilated greenhouses and carbon dioxide? Sunny days and heat? Nighttime and heat? Ventilation and heat? Partly cloudy days and heat? Sunny days and water vapor? Nighttime and water vapor? Ventilation and water vapor? Cold weather and water vapor? Sunny days and air circulation? Nighttime and air circulation? Heating and air circulation? Ventilating and air circulation?

17. During cold weather what is the effect on air components by starting the heating system before sunset and then continuing venting for awhile?

18. What is the relationship between soil air and soil water?

19. What season of the year is most difficult for maintaining the needed air supply in the soil?

20. What are the effects of heating on soil air and water relationships?

21. Why is air movement limited in propagating areas?

22. How is misting used in propagating areas?

Buildings, Greenhouse

1. What are some differences between greenhouses and conventional buildings?

2. What types of access do greenhouses need?

3. Why do greenhouse businesses need conventional as well as greenhouse buildings?

4. Why must decisions be made about type of crops, benching and walks, lighting, insulating, heating, and ventilation before the type of greenhouse can be chosen?

5. What are the differences between natural and fan ventilation systems?

6. What types of air circulation systems are used in greenhouses?

7. What are the needs for cut-flower and pot-plant benches, beds, and walks?

8. What qualities of coverings are considered before the start of greenhouse construction?

9. In what way does choice of covering affect choice of framework?

10. What is the main source of daytime heat in greenhouses?

11. Where is heating-system heat generated in greenhouses?

12. What equipment in greenhouses is used for regulation of light?

13. Why do greenhouse businesses need emergency electric generators?

14. What is a greenhouse bay?

15. Where are greenhouse trusses located?

16. Where are greenhouse gutters located?

17. What are the differences between greenhouse sideposts and gutterposts?

18. How are greenhouse roofs supported?

19. What are the differences between supplemental lighting and photoperiodic lighting?

20. What provisions are made for maximum admittance of sunlight into greenhouses?

21. What provisions are made for reducing the amount of sunlight for some crops?

22. What equipment is needed to supply long photoperiods during naturally short photoperiods?

23. What equipment is needed to supply short photoperiods during naturally long photoperiods?

24. In the United States and Canada, what are the seasons for naturally short photoperiods? Naturally long photoperiods?

25. How are heating and water pipelines installed in greenhouses?

26. What equipment is needed for the control of heating, ventilating, and irrigating: Manually? Electrically? Electronically?

27. Why is refrigerating equipment needed in greenhouse businesses?

28. How is heat distributed in propagating areas?

29. Are greenhouse buildings needed for propagating plants?

30. If greenhouse buildings are used for propagating, in what ways are the surroundings changed from the surroundings used for the production of plants and flowers?

Crops

1. Where in the United States and Canada is the main area for the production of carnation flowers?

2. What crop starters are used for carnation flower crops?

3. Why are the crop starters usually purchased from propagation specialists?

4. How are carnation rooted cuttings planted?

5. Why are carnation rooted cuttings planted this way?

6. How are carnation plants pinched?

7. What temperatures and photoperiods are used for carnation plants?

8. What procedures are used to avoid disease of carnation plants?

9. How are standard carnation cultivars disbudded?

10. How are miniature carnation cultivars disbudded?

11. How are carnation flowers harvested?

12. What pests are common with carnation plants, and how can these pests be observed?

13. What crop starters are used for iris flower crops?

14. How are iris crop starters planted?

15. How are iris flowers harvested?

16. Where in the United States and Canada are the main areas of chrysanthemum flower production?

17. How are crop starters planted for chrysanthemum flower crops?

18. What is the length of cropping time for chrysanthemum flower crops from planting to harvest, and how are succeeding flower crops produced?

19. What temperatures and photoperiods are needed for chrysanthemum flower production?

20. What procedures are used to avoid diseases with chrysanthemum flower crops?

21. What pests are common with chrysanthemum plants, and how can these pests be observed?

22. How are chrysanthemum flowers harvested?

23. What are the advantages in producing rose flower crops close to flower markets?

24. What crop starters are used for rose flower production, and how are these crop starters planted?

25. Where in the United States and Canada are rose crop starters produced?

26. How many years are rose plants kept in flower production?

27. How are rose stems pinched?

28. What temperatures and photoperiods are used for rose flower production?

29. How is the amount of rose flower production controlled for the projected marketing?

30. What pests and pathogens are common with rose plants, and how can the presence of pests and pathogens be observed?

31. How are rose flowers harvested?

32. What kinds of wholesale marketing are used for cut flowers in the United States and Canada?

33. What crop starters are used for snapdragon flower crops?

34. What temperatures and photoperiods are used for snapdragon flower production?

35. What types of wholesale marketing of pot plants are used in the United States and Canada?

36. What crop starters are used for African violet pot-plant production?

37. What temperatures and light conditions are used for African violet pot-plant production?

38. What temperatures are used for azalea pot-plant production?

39. How are chrysanthemum pot-plant crop starters potted?

40. What temperatures and photoperiods are used for pot mums?

41. What procedures are used to avoid disease in pot-mum crops?

42. What times of the year are pot-mum crops produced?

43. What methods of irrigation are used for cut-flower crops?

44. What methods of irrigation are used for pot-plant crops?

45. How and when are pot mums pinched?

46. Why are pot mums pinched?

47. What pot-plant crops are started from seed?

48. What pot-plant crops are started from bulbs or corms?

49. How are geranium propagated?

50. How are poinsettia propagated?

51. What temperatures and photoperiods are used for Easter lily pot-plants?

52. How are poinsettia crop starters potted?

53. What temperatures and photoperiods are used for poinsettia pot plants?

54. What procedures are used to avoid poinsettia diseases?

55. What differences in growth would there be between pot mums grown only in short photoperiods and pot mums grown only in long photo-periods?

56. What differences in growth would there be between African violet pot plants grown either in long or short photoperiods?

57. Would a poinsettia pot plant grown only in long photoperiods flower for Christmas?

58. What is the relationship in each plant of growth of roots and stems?

59. How do pot-plant growers observe root growth?

60. Why do pot-plant growers observe root growth?

61. When is pot-to-pot spacing used with pot-plant crops?

62. What are the reasons for spacing pot-plant crops during production?

63. Why is it more difficult to plan the use of a greenhouse area with pot-plant crops than with cut-flower crops?

Growth

1. What parts of the greenhouse surroundings affect plant growth?

2. Why do the roots of greenhouse plants fail to grow in waterlogged soils?

3. What are the differences between propagating and reproducing greenhouse plants?

4. What kinds of plant growth occur during propagation?

5. What are the advantages of bushy-type growth of greenhouse plants?

6. What are some greenhouse plants that have bushy (selfbranching) growth?

7. What procedures do greenhouse growers use to cause plants to branch?

8. Do greenhouse growers pinch selfbranching plants? Explain.

9. What greenhouse plants have terminal flowers?

10. What greenhouse plants have lateral flowers?

11. Why do terminal flowers have leafy stems?

12. What may cause malformed growth?

13. What is mutation of growth?

14. How does the amount of carbon dioxide in the air affect plant growth?

15. In general, how does decrease in temperature affect plant growth?

16. Why do greenhouse plants need food?

17. What effect may hormones have on plant growth?

18. Why do plants need a continuous supply of oxygen?

19. What greenhouse plants have better growth with increases in the amount of light?

20. What greenhouse plants have better growth with moderate amounts of light?

21. What type of growth does rose have in long photoperiods?

22. What type of growth does rose have in short photoperiods?

23. In what ways may pests affect plant growth?

24. Can the presence of some pests be suspected because of certain variations in plant growth? Explain.

25. In what ways may pathogens affect plant growth?

26. What kinds of plant growth may be affected by manufactured regulators?

27. What effects may variations in minerals have on plant growth?

28. How is plant growth affected by pinching?

29. How is plant growth affected by disbudding?

30. How is plant growth affected by waterlogged soil?

31. How is plant growth affected by lack of water in soils?

32. How is plant growth affected by too much water vapor in the air?

33. During what type of plant growth is more moisture added to the air?

34. How can greenhouse surroundings be adjusted for various stages of plant growth?

35. What are some causes of curvature of stem growth?

36. What greenhouse plants have long stems?

37. What greenhouse plants have short (compact) stems?

38. What procedures can be used to produce greenhouse crops with longer stems?

39. What type of greenhouse crops may be improved with longer stems?

40. What procedures may be used to produce greenhouse crops with shorter stems?

41. What type of greenhouse crops may be improved with shorter stems?

42. What procedures may be used to produce greenhouse crops with larger flowers?

43. What procedures may be used to produce a greater number of flowers per unit area?

44. What plant growth differences are there between propagation by stem-tip cuttings and propagation by leaf cuttings?

45. What plant growth differences are there between propagation by stem-tip cuttings and propagation by seed?

46. Why is it important to use pathogen-free stock in propagation?

47. What are stock plants?

48. What qualities are needed in propagating soils?

Plant Characteristics

1. What term may be used for the aboveground part of greenhouse plants?

2. In what ways do underground stems differ from roots?

3. In what ways are aboveground and underground stems similar?

4. What is vegetative growth, and how does it differ from reproductive growth?

5. What are the differences between determinate and indeterminate growth?

6. Where do leaves originate?

7. Where do flowers originate?

8. Where do branches originate?

9. In what ways are aboveground and underground stems different?

10. How do leaves in greenhouse plants differ?

11. Can the various greenhouse plants be distinguished just by leaf characteristics? Explain.

12. What greenhouse plants have only aboveground stems?

13. What greenhouse plants have bisexual flowers?

14. What greenhouse plants are known mainly for their underground stems?

15. What greenhouse plants have unisexual flowers?

16. Which florets develop first in chrysanthemum?

17. Which florets develop first in geranium?

18. Which florets develop first in snapdragon?

19. Why must plant roots grow continuously?

20. How do plants reproduce?

21. What is vegetative reproduction?

22. What is the relationship of plants reproduced vegetatively?

23. What is the relationship of plants reproduced sexually?

24. What is the most common color of greenhouse plant stems and leaves?

25. What causes the color of greenhouse plants?

26. What food is produced by plants?

27. Why is it necessary for greenhouse plants to be in light?

28. What is transpiration?

29. Why do plants wilt?

30. Why do plants need dissolved fertilizers?

31. What are air pollutants?

32. What are the effects of some air pollutants on plants?

33. What effect does plant color have on the entry of light into plants?

34. What is a blind shoot?

INDEX

H

I